Solitary Witch

Common Sense Magic

For beginners, people who want to enhance, advance, or refresh their practice, and those who like to be different!

Liz Pilley

CAPALL BANN PUBLISHING

www.capallbann.co.uk

Solitary Eclectic Witchcraft

Cover design by Paul Mason

Published by:

Capall Bann Publishing
Auton Farm
Milverton
Somerset
TA4 1NE

Contents

Introduction

What is Eclectic Witchcraft?

E clectic Witchcraft is very difficult to define. As with all forms of Witchcraft, different people have different ideas of what it means to them. What is outlined in this book can only ever be my opinion, my interpretation and my ideas of how to practise Witchcraft in the twenty-first century.

In some ways, it is easier to state what Eclectic Witchcraft is not: it is not Wicca as would be understood by a traditional Gardnerian or Alexandrian, although it can be combined with either of these paths; it is not about following rules or set rituals; it is not about following someone else's idea of what religion should be about. Eclectic Witchcraft is for rebels and free-thinkers. It is for people who do not like to be told what to think, what to do, or how to do it. If you like to read books on Witchcraft but always adapt the ideas to suit yourself, then Eclectic Witchcraft may be for you.

If you are not afraid of studying many different traditions and then experimenting until you find what works for you, then you may be a natural Eclectic. This is not to say that Eclectic Witchcraft is a softer substitute for the learning and discipline found in more formal traditions – far from it. In order to find what works for you, you will need a broad range of knowledge that can only come from study, experience and trial-and-error. You may often find your commitment and discipline tested by difficult times in order that you may learn to help others through similar hardships. The more deeply you immerse yourself in this style of Witchcraft, the more aware you will become of such occurrences.

A question often asked is: what is the difference between Witchcraft and Wicca? My interpretation is that Wicca is a mystical, fairly formal religious system complete in itself, while Witchcraft is a framework for practising magic and a way of looking at the world; a catch-all term for folk who practise magic of all sorts and flavours. Therefore a Witch need not believe in a God and Goddess and indeed, may not even be Pagan or have any religious beliefs at all. In this book, I shall be attempting to show how you can combine a practice of Eclectic Witchcraft with Pagan beliefs and why the two go together so well, but it should be borne in mind that magic can be practised without this spiritual aspect.

Many books on Wicca start with a short history of the path, including the medieval witch-hunts, late-nineteenth century spiritualist and occult revival, and of course Gerald Gardner and Alex Sanders. A lot of this history is much-disputed and, although an interesting subject for research and discussion, it is not directly relevant to modern-day practice. A spiritual path does not need to have a long history to be valid and effective, and you do not need to try and find 'the truth' about Witchcraft's history in order to be a Witch today.

Another subject I shall not be covering is listings of magical correspondences – items such as herbs, colours, trees which are associated with particular spells or desired outcomes. Again, this is because this subject is much-disputed and if you read several different books covering this topic, they will often give you different associations depending on the magical system upon which they are based. I am not suggesting you should make things up as you go along – instead, read up on as many different systems as you can until you find correspondences which appeal to you. This is the whole point of symbolism and association: it is supposed to be a shorthand for your mind. Therefore, it is no good doing a spell for good health using a green candle, if in your subconscious you associate green with nausea. Instead, study different people's suggestions of magical correspondences until you find one you agree with, or until it gives you the confidence to try out a correspondence which is entirely new but which may work for you.

Eclectic Witchcraft is usually practised alone or with a partner rather than in a coven. This is not because Eclectic Witches don't believe in covens, but because it can be hard to find other people who practise in exactly the same way or who are prepared to compromise their understanding of Witchcraft with the understanding of others'. Eclectic Witchcraft can be a lonely path, needing great strength of character and self-confidence. Although it is without rules and can be adapted for each practitioner, this does not make it an easy option. You must be prepared to work very hard on yourself, often without the support of like-minded individuals that a coven can bring. It requires discipline and study to gain the best results and you will need the strength of mind and confidence in yourself to practise as you see fit, often against the criticism and even hostility of other Witches who practise more formally. In this book, I will be covering many subjects that do not at first glance seem directly connected with Witchcraft - personal development and responsibility for example - but the study of these subjects is vital to prepare yourself for the practice of magic and for the development of your personal power. You could practise without learning these skills, but your personal power would be much weaker and less focused and there would be the danger of doing accidental harm to yourself and others through ignorance.

I view Witchcraft as a vocation similar to being a healer or philosopher. It is a way of living which is connected to earth and community, family and friendship. There are many benefits of being a Witch – you learn about yourself and others, gain wisdom and understanding, and feel balanced, focused and connected to the earth. You have the satisfaction of constantly learning new things, helping others and feeling a sense of fulfilment. It may not make you rich or conventionally successful, but you have a far greater chance of happiness. As you learn to take responsibility for your actions, so your sense of personal power and control will grow giving you a sense of security in an uncertain world. You will understand how best to make necessary changes to your life and how to calmly accept things which you cannot affect and for which you are not responsible.

Witchcraft is a nature-based way of working and as such it aims to have an earth-centred approach to life which can be challenging in this day and age, especially in an urban setting. This is more than just recycling your newspapers, it requires a whole new approach to life which could change it radically. Only you can decide how far you are willing or able to go with this, but it is a central part of the Witch's philosophy and one that is often overlooked in modern books on Witchcraft which focus mainly on spells and magic. This is self-defeating as the power for spells and magic comes from your connection with the earth which only an earth-centredness can bring. The healing aspect is also often left out although this is another huge part of what Witchcraft is. The reason you spend so much time learning is so that you can share this knowledge to help yourself and others, in a similar way to traditional 'cunning folk' or 'wise-women' – this can include therapies as well as advice, friendship, magical and non-magical help.

This book aims to provide a practical programme for starting out in Eclectic Witchcraft giving both food for thought and exercises to complete. It doesn't tell you what to think, worship, or believe but instead gives you the tools to work out these things for yourself in an individual programme. Witchcraft is not a 'fluffy' New-Age option, it is a serious path requiring commitment and effort, but by putting that extra amount in, you get so much more out.

Chapter 1

Preparing Yourself for Witchcraft

Before starting this chapter, it might be worth investing in a good notebook, diary or journal. I have included lots of practical exercises to do to develop your power and prepare yourself for Witchcraft and it will be useful to keep the results of these to look back on. You may well find yourself wanting to keep some sort of diary or journal to chart your progress and note down important insights, thoughts or dreams. You can call this a Book of Shadows or Grimoire if it seems appropriate to you, as it will be a place to record magical progress, but don't make it too formal or you will find yourself wanting to leave out random jottings or make corrections, and it is important that you don't do this, for mistakes are important records of progress too. Your notebook should be somewhere to:

- Make a note of someone you want to send healing to;

- Record how you felt on a day when you were really happy;

- Write down the name of a book someone recommends;

- Press a flower in;

- Draw a sketch of a loved one;

- List the herbs you want to cultivate next spring.

- And anything and everything else!

It could be hand-written, a computer disk, a ringbinder – whichever feels right to you.

Balance

It is often said that balance is the key to power, and nowhere is this more true than within yourself. If you are out of balance, your power will be off-balance, unfocused and generally weaker than if you are perfectly tuned. So, how do you become balanced and maintain that balance? There is no simple answer. Only you can discover your own balance and it takes time, concentration and discipline. It is easy to let yourself become unbalanced even once you are aware of the issue – this is when you start to feel that 'things are getting on top of you' or get a nagging feeling that something is wrong but you are not sure what. Things such as jobs, schoolwork, family and domestic responsibilities seem to 'drown out' your spiritual voice and you wonder when you'll ever get time for 'me' again. But, as with all complicated things, if you break it down into smaller steps, it becomes more manageable, and there are plenty of practical exercises you can do to help.

Exercise

• Write down all the things you do each day – every task you complete no matter how mundane – and the time it takes you to do them. At the end of one week, you will have built up a diary of a fairly typical week in your life and the activities which fill your days. Take four differently coloured pens or highlighters and mark each item in a different colour according to the following system: 1st colour – things you don't like doing but are necessary for living, such as cleaning, washing clothes. 2nd colour – tasks you do not actively enjoy but to which you have committed yourself for other benefits, such as homework, emptying the cat's litter tray, taking your child to ballet lessons. 3rd colour – things you don't like doing but are expected to do, either by your family or friends or by society in general, such as hosting dinner parties, attending awkward family events, trimming your hedge. 4th colour – things you actively enjoy doing and have freely chosen to do.

Look at your diary of tasks and note which colour predom-inates. This is an easy way of seeing where you expend the most energy and where you need to make some effort to re-establish your balance. If you spend the most amount of time on necessary tasks, ask yourself if they are really necessary? Do you cling to a higher state of cleanliness in your house than is really necessary simply because that is how you have been brought up? Do other adults in the house do their fair share of chores? If not, how could you negotiate so that they do, without causing anger and ill-feeling? Can you give small tasks to children, or larger tasks to older children, for example making the children responsible for one family meal a week? This could be negotiated as a trade-off for increased freedoms on their part – they do their own ironing but are allowed to come home an hour later in the evening.

If tasks which you have committed yourself to for future benefits predominate, then look carefully if you may have over-committed yourself. For example, if you are devoting a lot of time to studying because you will value the future qualification, then you may have to postpone some other current commitments in the short-term in order to give your best to the studying. And rather than feeling grumpy about missing out, try to remind yourself that this was your active decision, which is something to feel good about. You are in control. Obviously, if your current commitments are children or animals, you can't simply cancel them if you feel overwhelmed, but you can ask for help in their care, from partners, family or friends. If you spend all your time ferrying different children to different activities ask yourself how much they really get out of these activities? Is it more important to you than them that they learn karate or the piano? Might you both get more out of spending some quiet time at home reading together or doing a jigsaw puzzle or going for a short walk? Can you set up schemes with others so that you all get a break sometimes from constant picking up and dropping off?

Other people's expectations can easily take over your life and it can be difficult to get away from these, especially if we do not want to let others down or upset them. But in the long-run it will be better for everyone if you can be honest. If your parents have always wanted you to be the first in the family to go to university but you are just not an academic person, tell them. But do it in a constructive way – don't accuse them of pushing you into something you don't want to do, instead formulate an action plan for what you want to do instead and be enthusiastic and positive about it. All parents want is their children's happiness and although they may be disappointed, it will be better to be honest as early on as possible. Maybe you feel you are expected to be the perfect wife and mother, but you would rather be back at work, or you feel expected to be a career-man when you would rather be a musician or artist. It can be hard to go against society's expectations of studying, gaining a well-paid 9-5 job and settling down to produce a family, but try and think creatively. Can you create your ideal life with something a little more unconventional? Could you work part-time in a steady job and follow your creative dreams part-time? Can you remind people who expect things from you, that these things are not your dreams, but theirs and that you have no obligation to follow them?

If the things you actively enjoy predominate, then well done! For most people this will be the category with the fewest things in it. Many of us feel guilty at putting ourselves first and if time is short, will always satisfy everyone else's demands first, often short-changing ourselves in the process. I'm not suggesting you become completely selfish and ignore everyone else's needs, just that you gain a balance between your responsibilities, chores and pleasures. You will perform your other tasks better if you have taken the time to relax, recharge and follow your own pursuits, and you will be spared the temptation to play the martyr. You need not whine or argue in your attempts to gain some me-time, simply state your intentions firmly and definitely, for example 'I am going to have a long bath and I will be locking the door.' It is very tempting to think that you cannot possibly find any time for this kind of indulgence, but if you look through all the tasks you have written down during the week, it would be very surprising if you could not find just an extra 5 or 10 minutes for yourself.

Look through the whole list again and give yourself a large pat on the back for everything you've achieved in one week.

Finðing youꞛ Path
Each of us has a path in life that we are meant to follow, a purpose we are meant to fulfil, or a lesson we are meant to learn, for example, teaching, healing or patience. For some people, finding this can be a lifetime's work but others know from an early age what it is they are meant to do. Some of us feel we are meant to be doing something but are not sure what exactly, and so flit from thing to thing trying to find our purpose. Some of us don't feel we have a predestined purpose and so need to define for ourselves what our purpose is in this life. Whichever type of person you are, you cannot be in a true balance if you are on the wrong path.

10

In today's world it is easy to be led astray by the constant bombardment of marketing advertising the latest products and the glamorous lives of celebrities. It is easy to think that you could be happier if only you were richer or thinner, had a bigger house or a bigger car, or the latest games console. Some people reject these kind of values outright and try self-sufficiency in a rural setting, and while this is a valid option, it would not suit all of us. Many people feel caught between two worlds as we cannot completely reject the trappings of the modern world and yet want to live in a more spiritually fulfilling way. For many people, finding this compromise can be the key to finding their paths in life, and feeling happier and more fulfilled.

Exercise

- Imagine you have won the Lottery. (I should add here that this exercise is not actually about money, merely that lack of money is something which inhibits the dreams of many people.) As children, we dream of outlandish things we'd like to do when we grow up, like fly or become a dog, but as we grow up we realise that everything costs money and we downsize our dreams in line with this realisation. But this inhibition can actually block us from finding our true path in life. Therefore, imagining we have won a vast fortune frees the imagination to soar in childish freedom again. Freed from having to work to pay the rent and feed ourselves, what would we truly enjoy? Start writing things down. Don't worry about keeping it neat or practical, just write whatever comes into your mind.

- Would you give up working or would you start your own form of business or organisation?

- Would you found a donkey sanctuary or backpack round the world for three years?

- Would you have ten children or none?

- Would you give some money away or invest it in your own vision?

- Would you study or go on holiday?

- Would you buy a house or leave the country?

All these things tell you a huge amount about the kind of person you are and the things which are important to you. If you'd travel, your freedom is important to you and you like to experience things firsthand. If you'd buy a farm and raise chickens, your roots and security are important to you and you like to feel connected to the land. Maybe you'd be an artist or write a novel; maybe you'd volunteer for some sort of charity. Whatever your thoughts, they can tell you a lot about the kind of path you should be seeking.

Now is the time to come back to earth. Unfortunately, most of us won't win the Lottery, but that doesn't mean we can't put our dreams into action. We just have to start small. If you dreamt of opening an animal sanctuary, could you find out about working for an animal shelter, even if it's only for an hour a week as a volunteer? If you dreamt of going around the world, could you start saving for a two week visit to the country which excites you the most or volunteer for Voluntary Services Overseas or other schemes for working abroad? If you wanted to study or re-train, is there a way you could do it part-time or by distance learning, or could you afford to do it full-time if you saved up first? Many things are actually possible once you start thinking about them carefully and making detailed plans. Sometimes it is hard to embark on plans which may take five or six years or even longer to come to fruition, but there is only one thing certain here – if you don't embark on them at all, you will definitely never reach the goal. Starting out on a long road takes you that bit closer to your finishing point.

Being Happy

You might wonder what being happy has to do with Witchcraft, but it has a great deal to do with your personal power and focus. A Witch who is unhappy in her own skin and dissatisfied with her life is a loose cannon, and is someone who is tempted to use unethical magic to get more of what she wants in her life. She is also someone who is no help for healing others. Being unhappy or negative takes up a lot of energy and will leave you with none left over to give to others who need your help. You shouldn't even try to heal others if you have lots of outstanding issues yourself, as you will leave yourself dangerously short of energy for dealing with your own problems and may harm more than you help other people. Always try to be at full-strength and full-balance before you give of yourself to others.

Unfortunately, there are no short-cuts to happiness, but it is easier to be happy than most people think. The main myth about being happy is that you have no control over it. Most people think that if sad or nasty things happen to you, you will be unhappy and if nice things happen to you, you will be happy. And to a certain extent this is true, as external events obviously influence our mood on a day-to-day basis. But we all must know people to whom awful things have happened, and yet they seem to cope well and keep an inner sense of contentment through the worst times. It is easy to be envious or dismissive of these people, feeling that they must have just been 'born lucky' or that they have had more help in life than you have. But this may not be the case, it may well be that these kind of people just have a different outlook on life than someone who feels less happy. It is a myth that some people are lucky or unlucky – everyone will experience some good events and some adverse events in their lives. It all depends on your interpretation of these events. Someone who thinks of themselves as a lucky person will tend to dwell on the good things that happen while someone who thinks of themselves as an unlucky or 'cursed' person will tend to dwell on the bad.

If you think you are lucky, you will also tend to seize opportunities that come your way as you will assume they will turn out well. People who presume they are unlucky will worry more about possible negative outcomes and may talk themselves out of taking up a good opportunity. It may sometimes be hard to see it, but the universe tends to provide what we need at any particular time. For example, when you are thinking about taking a new job, you may suddenly see articles in magazines or items on television programmes about people starting new jobs. This may just be coincidence, or it may be more than that, but take notice of these messages and try to let them help you decide the best course of action.

When it comes to other people, there is a huge gulf between your perception of them and their reality. They may seem confident and clever and all the other things that you wish you were yourself, but maybe that person is looking at you and thinking the same thing. Everyone has a mask or public persona, but this does not always represent how they truly feel, just as you may not always publicly show your true feelings. It is worth remembering that you do not see what people are feeling inside, you don't see if they cry at night and you don't see the effort it costs them to stay calm and deal with things well. They are just as human as you, with the same doubts, insecurities and sadnesses, but they have learned a skill to cope with life and you can learn it too. This isn't to say that you will go around with a broad grin on your face all the time, mindlessly cheerful, but you will be able to learn to feel more satisfied with life and optimistic for the future.

Low self-esteem and lack of confidence can be real problems, but are luckily the sort of problems which can be worked on. Generally, low self-esteem comes from having a skewed vision of yourself as bad at everything or as someone that nobody likes. If you talk to other people about how they view you though, you may be surprised. You may think that you can't cope with life or you have a bad temper or you are unlikeable, but other people may see you as a calm, happy and amicable person. This can be quite a surprise. In the same way, you should realise that another person whom you admire as having all the qualities you wish you possessed, may themselves think they are useless. If you can try this out for yourself and talk to someone it can be a huge step to improving your self-esteem and self-confidence.

The first thing to do is try to find balance in your life – just achieving that, even if it is only sometimes – will make you feel more in control and therefore happier. Also, finding or working towards your path in life will make you feel more comfortable with yourself at a subconscious level. The next thing to do may be a huge thing, but it is worth doing. Most of us have experienced some sort of trauma in our lives whether it is the death of a loved one, some sort of abuse, eating disorder, depression or health problem. All these things can leave their mark very deeply, but they can be worked through. Whatever pain you are going through or have been through, remember you are never alone – others will have suffered in a similar way and can help you on the road to recovery. Ask for help if you need it. Don't soldier on when people are willing and able to assist – that is just self-defeating. If you have some sort of current or past problem, face up to it and deal with it with appropriate support. You will never be able to move on unless you do so, and you deserve to move on – you deserve to be happy. Whatever you have experienced, you are not to blame and neither is the world – so don't reject yourself or the world. But you can take control now.

Exercise

- What makes you happy? Write a list or spider diagram. It could be simple things like music, 'Eastenders', sunshine, or more complicated things like a day out learning to skydive. If you can't think of abstract things which make you happy, then write down times in the past when you've been happy, such as last year's birthday party, or 'when I got an 'A' for my essay'. Write down as many as you can think of. When you have finished, look through what you have written. What is it about these things which makes you happy? Is it a simple sensual pleasure such as the taste of chocolate? Or is it something more complex such as a sense of belonging to a family, or a feeling of freedom from ordinary responsibilities?

How many of these pleasure-giving activities have you done in the last week? How many could you do next week? Why don't you? If your main pleasures are social, can you spend more time with friends or family? If you enjoy special food, could you go on a cookery course?

Aim to do at least five things from your list in the week and see how it makes you feel at the end of the week.

The next step is to start changing your attitude. What you put out into the world is what you get back. You can see it happening all around you. People who are always complaining always seem to get something to complain about whereas people who are generally contented seem to receive good luck. This can be a very powerful spell – if you dwell on all the bad consequences that could arise from something, then they can be more likely to happen. If you concentrate on positive outcomes, they will be more likely. Every time something not-so-good happens to you and you catch yourself thinking 'typical!', stop and imagine a positive outcome instead. Break the cycle of thinking of yourself as an unlucky person – you are simply a person who has sometimes had some bad things happen in their life, and sometimes had some good things happen. Remember that it is much easier to remember the bad things – if need be, write down every time something good happens so that you start to remember these things just as much, if not more, than the bad ones.

When you have a specific task to do like an exam or a driving test, take the time beforehand to visualise yourself passing and celebrating your achievement. If you don't pass this time, think about what you have learned which will make it all the more likely you will pass next time, rather than dwelling on the whole experience as a failure and then giving up.

Exercise

- Learn to appreciate the little things in life. Life is filled with everyday magic which we don't notice because we're too busy, too negative, or have become used to it. Learn to wonder at small things in the way children do. The sunshine, birds singing, the taste of a favourite food, the comfort of a warm bed on a cold night, putting your feet up with a cup of tea after a long day. Cultivate little moments of humour in your day. When something strikes you as funny, have a small chuckle and remember it to share with a partner or friend later in the day, so that you can enjoy it again.

Add some lightness to your life – instead of seeing the latest horror film, catch a comedy. You'll feel better for it. Read a funny book, watch a funny programme on the television. Let yourself be silly sometimes – go to the park and kick up a great pile of autumn leaves, have a snowball fight or a water fight. Lie on your back on the floor and wave your legs in the air – encourage your whole family to join you!

Learn to catch yourself as you start thinking negative thoughts. Ask yourself why you thought that, and substitute the opposite, positive thought instead. If low self-esteem is causing you to think negatively, then do some specific work on that area. Think of all the things that you do well or are good at. Write a list of all your achievements, no matter how small. Keep a special section in your journal for writing down every time you receive a compliment or positive comment, for example when a boss or teacher praises you, when your cat chooses your lap to sit in all evening, when your child hugs you, when your best mate tells you you're looking well. Every time you start to think negatively about yourself, get out your journal and look at this section to remind yourself that other people think you're great. Don't forget to ask other people for help in this area too: sit down with a trusted friend, partner or parent and ask them what they think you're good at and why they value you. You may be surprised at the kinds of things they say and discover that other people see you in an entirely different light than you see yourself.

Practise What You Preach

No-one likes a hypocrite but it is easy to be hypocritical yourself without realising it. In espousing Witchcraft, you are committing yourself to a lifestyle which should be different from the average material-focused way of living. Witches respect the earth and draw power from living as far as possible in harmony with their natural surroundings. Witches also have different goals from the conventional ones of acquiring money and possessions – goals such as love, honour, and healing. However, living in the twenty-first century, especially in a town or city, it is easy to be sucked into not practising what you preach and becoming the kind of Witch who spends ages organising a Samhain ritual but who otherwise lives a consumerist lifestyle which is highly wasteful of the resources of our planet. I am not suggesting that everyone should 'drop out' of modern life and become a traveller or live in a tent in a field close to nature, but I am suggesting that all of us could do more to respect the earth than we are currently doing, and that good intentions are often over-ridden by the day-to-day concerns of family life or a busy career (or both!).

I could easily list a whole load of simple ways of becoming greener in your lifestyle, such as recycling waste, composting, insulating your house, buying items with less packaging – but these suggestions are probably familiar to all of us. What I am thinking of is challenging our mindsets for what is necessary in life. We all have a threshold over which we feel we 'cannot' step. For example, many people will buy unleaded petrol but how many will seriously consider living without a car? We may try to buy organic, but how many of us will actually grow our own food? We may feel strongly about energy conservation but will we refuse to buy a dishwasher on those grounds? What I am trying to ask here is this: how many of us are actually willing to deny ourselves or make life more difficult for ourselves on the grounds of living up to our (supposedly) earth-honouring principles?

Exercise

- It is time to think seriously about some of these examples. To start with: cars. In Western culture, learning to drive and buying a first car has become something of a rite of passage, especially for young men. If you are starting a first job, people may ask you when you'll be getting a car, and if you have not learnt to drive, some people may find this peculiar. But do you really need a car? People have all sorts of reasons for needing a car. Women cite safety reasons and fear of using public transport, parents cite the necessity of transporting off-spring in comfort and safety, many people give the reason that it is the cheapest method of transport, or that they need it to get to work. And these reasons may be true, or they may be excuses because you have reached your comfort threshold and are not willing to step over it. Only you can decide which it is. But spend some time thinking about your reasoning. Is public transport where you live really unsafe? Do other people you know use it perfectly happily? If you commute a long distance to work, why do you do this? Could you find work closer to home or live closer to work? Could you work from home? Could you have shopping delivered or take a taxi to do one big shop per month? Could you share a car with a friend or family member? Once you take into account the cost of buying the car, insuring it, taxing it, maintaining it and filling it with petrol, is it really the cheapest transport option for you? The answers to all these questions will depend on your own particular circumstances and where you live, and no-one should judge you on your replies, but if you are very honest with yourself, maybe you will find that you don't so much need a car as want one, and you may want to do something about that.

Jobs are another huge area of life where principles can easily go out of the window. Many people compartmentalise their lives, putting their spirituality on one side and their career on the other. For people who fear discrimination in their work if they are open about their religious beliefs, this may be a necessity but for others it has just become a way of life because they see the two areas as totally separate. I'm not advocating going in to work constantly talking about your beliefs nor even mentioning them, but instead thinking about how your career impinges on your beliefs in subtle ways.

Do you work such long hours that you find it hard to get the time or energy to spend on religious (or any other) activities? Does your work require you to do things or act in a way that is incompatible with your core beliefs, such as promoting products you believe to be harmful to the environment or doing contract work for the Ministry of Defence if you are a pacifist? Do you feel that you 'become another person' while you're at work? If so, you really need to look hard at whether this job suits you. For many people, it is very hard or even unthinkable to change styles of job. We are brought up to believe that once we leave school, we work full-time until we retire unless we have a break to bring up a family. For many people, part-time work, contract work or self-employment are options too risky to consider. But there are many more flexible options to working these days. There are grants and courses to help you follow that dream to work for yourself.

Many people spend a lot of time working hard in order to finance labour-saving devices which they wouldn't need if they weren't working such long hours. Full-time and part-time aren't such rigid options as they once were. It may be possible to cut down just a few hours a week on your work commitment in order to have that time to yourself you so desperately need. It may be blocks in your own mind-set which are preventing you from seeing such an option. Sit down and work out where all your money goes – how much of it do you spend on takeaways or ready-meals when you're too tired to cook? How much is wasted on material items you don't really need but which 'cheer you up' or compensate you for working so hard. Do your children really need or want so many new clothes and toys, do you really need a new sofa or car? A good way of working out where the money goes is to keep a log of how much you spend and what on for a month. Include the cost of bills, rent or mortgage and find out a realistic monthly budget. You may be surprised how much you spend on some things and find that you can easily cut down on these items, giving you more money to play with. Families are expensive to maintain, but sometimes they are not as expensive as you think if you take the time to appreciate the simpler things and to say 'no' to the more material and consumerist-led ones.

Do you give anything back to your community? This is another tricky one as it involves giving time and giving of yourself rather than just putting money in a collecting tin. Do you know anything about the area you live in? Have you learnt anything about its history and character? Do you join in with any local events such as fetes or fairs? Do you support your local shops and businesses? Could your neighbours knock on your door if they needed help? Do you ever volunteer your time to a local school or organisation? Do you have skills which you could donate? Do you pick up litter when you go to your local park? All of these are ways of giving something back to your local community, and they are all rewarding ways of becoming more of a part of your local community at the same time.

I'm sure there are many other examples you can think of and hopefully these exercises will help you question the assumptions you make about what is necessary in your life. If you are a teenager and currently have little control over these aspects of your life, spend some time thinking about how you'd like your future lifestyle to be. Can you make some suggestions to your parents for improvements to the family's lifestyle now, for example, could you volunteer to take the family's glass to the recycler once a week? Think carefully about the subjects you study at school and the kind of job you are hoping to have one day – is it the kind of thing that fits in with your beliefs or does it contradict them? For example, if you mean to study Business Studies and then work in the City, does this fit in with a lifestyle which is non-material and earth-honouring? If it does not, is there a way you could make it so, or could you slightly alter your plans to make it fit your beliefs?

The whole point is to make your spiritual beliefs a part of every aspect of your life, something that you put into practice (or at least try to) 24 hours a day, seven days a week - not just on the major festival days. Witchcraft should be more than just celebrating festivals, it should be about living differently, caring and healing, valuing something other than having the latest hi-fi or car.

This is not about feeling guilty, just about thinking about your actions. You may feel that you are already doing everything you can and living your beliefs as fully as you can, and that's fine. The key thing is to think about it periodically and re-assess your life. It is easy to slip into bad habits and with major life changes such as getting married, leaving university or having children, there will be different pressures on you and different decisions to make about how far you are comfortable with having an alternative lifestyle. However, perhaps we should all be prepared to sacrifice a bit of comfort or a bit of time or money in order to live more simply and less hypocritically.

Keeping a Record

Keeping track of your progress is very important. Many of the exercises given involve writing things down, whether this be in lists, charts or notes. Until things are written down in black (or whatever colour!) and white on the page, it is easy to overlook things or not see patterns and connections which exist. For this reason, sometimes it can be useful to do an exercise, keep your responses and then repeat it several months later. You may find that you get even more out of it a second time, or even that you get something entirely different out of it as you have made progress within the intervening time.

For the same reason, it can be very helpful to keep a diary or journal of your daily life. In this, you could note such things as:

- What you did;

- Who you saw;

- What the weather was like;

- What you ate and drank;

- How you felt (physically, mentally and emotionally);

- How you slept;

- Interaction with friends and family;

- What you observed;

- What you wish you had done differently;

- Any ideas you have.

It does not matter if you don't do this everyday. If you miss doing it for a while, don't give up thinking that there's no point. Even just writing it a few times year can tell you a lot. If you write down just one observation each day for a week you will have seven insights that you might not have had before. Or maybe you will note down helpful ideas which have occurred to you previously but have been forgotten because they were not recorded.

After several months, you can start looking back on what you have recorded and you may find patterns which can help you to change your life for the better. For example, you may find:

- A correlation between what you ate and how you felt physically;

- A link between your partner's behaviour and your emotional well-being;

- That lack of sleep affects you;

- That being with a certain friend is draining you;

- That you are someone who has sudden ideas out of the blue but then doesn't follow them through.

On a mundane level, you may find the cause of those troublesome migraines, or realise that you don't sleep enough. On a magical level, you may discover that you have psychic tendencies or that you are an empath (someone who tunes in to another person's moods and is therefore affected by the emotional states of those around them). Maybe you feel more powerful and in tune at certain times of the year and more like hibernating at others. You may discover patterns to your relationships with your family and friends, such as a particular argument being repeated but never resolved. You will definitely discover a lot about yourself, the type of person you are and how you react to things.

Knowledge is power. Once you know things about yourself, you can begin to change the things you do not like or that aren't helpful to you. Sometimes it may be easy to do this after you have seen your behaviour more clearly – it can even be amusing to realise how often you get cross because your partner leaves the toilet seat up. It may make you see your behaviour in a different light and decide that it doesn't really matter in the grand scheme of things. Or it may make you realise that it is part of a pattern in your partner's behaviour which is disrespectful and dismissive of you, and decide to tackle this rather than just arguing about the toilet seat for the fiftieth time. The interpretation is down to you. But putting words down on paper can make things much clearer to you – you can see yourself and your world as a stranger might see you.

Remember that your record doesn't have to be entirely written – it is good to include things such as pictures, photos, songs, cinema tickets. Things you have made and things you have come across which spoke to you are all equally valid inclusions in such a diary and will be powerful reminders when you come to look back later over your journal.

There are a couple of subjects which you may want to include in your journal that I have kept separate – dreams and compliments. It is very important to keep a record of these things and you may wish to include them in your main journal, but if you feel you may want to refer to them more often, it may be practical to keep them separate.

Keeping a note of your dreams can give you great insights, but I would caution against being too analytical. Sometimes dreams are just nonsense – our brains sorting through the detritus of the day or rehashing the last film we saw. The whole point of keeping a dream diary is in order to be able to pinpoint when they are something more, when they may be trying to tell you something. This can often be the case with recurring dreams, especially when you see a little more of the image each time the dream happens, or in dreams of loved ones who are no longer with us.

It can be worthwhile consulting a dictionary of symbols when trying to decipher a dream, but remember that your own symbolism maybe different to that in the book. The point is to try and understand what the images mean to you personally and construct your own unique dictionary of symbols. It can also be interesting to see if you dream more vividly during different phases of the moon, different seasons or different parts of the menstrual cycle. Remember that men have hormonal cycles too and recording your dreams might enable you to identify yours for the first time.

Some people think that they don't dream at all, but this isn't true. Everyone dreams but many people don't remember theirs. Most people can only remember dreams in detail when they first wake up, and for this reason it is good to write them down first thing in the morning. This can also be a useful morning meditation – a quiet time concentrating on a spiritual exercise and a time to gather your thoughts and wake up gently.

I have already talked about keeping a diary of compliments and again, this need not be a written diary. It could actually be a box filled with reminders of happy times and people who love you. This can include photos of nights out, invitations to parties or weddings, tickets and programmes for events visited and other mementoes. It is still important to write down any spoken compliments you receive however, as these are the ones which are hardest to remember but which can have the greatest power. Try to remember the exact words if you can, but a near approximation is still helpful. Write them on small post-it notes with details of who said it and when, and drop them into your compliments box and then when you need a lift, take one out randomly and read it.

When you do this, remember that other people also feel low and lacking in self-confidence, so make sure that you take your turn at complimenting other people. Tell people you love them, thank them for things they do for you, compliment them on their outfit or their skills at doing a specific task. Make this a habit, not only with friends and family, but with strangers – when people offer you a seat on the bus, when you've had good service in a shop, when someone goes out of their way to help you. Make sure that you spread positivity, not negativity. It is easier to believe and remember the bad about ourselves than the good, but we should remember both equally if we are to stay in balance.

End of Chapter Relaxation

Whenever you complete a task it is good to give yourself a small reward, especially if the task has been difficult, unpleasant or challenging. While I hope it has not been unpleasant to read this chapter, it may have been challenging if you have been doing all the exercises along the way. So, as a reward, try something new that you have always wanted to try – something small like a new kind of chocolate bar, a new sort of wine, or a television programme, a new restaurant or takeaway.

Trying something new or doing something familiar in a different way can add novelty to your day and make you appreciate something anew. If you'd like to take this further, you could try sitting in a different chair in the living room than you usually sit in and notice the different perspective it gives you. Paint the bedroom in a new and soothing colour. Use a different route to work or go and look round a shop you've never been in before. Perhaps buy a CD by a band you've never heard of just because you like the name or cover. Try a new colour of lipstick or a new brand of aftershave. Use a new recipe, or get someone else to cook the dinner – someone who doesn't usually!

It is easy to despise or ignore the everyday, but it is great to be able to notice once again just how good things are. Small changes or small rewards can be very effective.

Further Reading

Non-fiction

The Complete Idiot's Guide to Reaching Your Goals – Jeff Davidson (1999, Alpha Books).
Although a bit over-the-top at times, this book is a very readable and practical guide to changing your life and achieving those ambitions you've always cherished but felt you'd never be able to actually do. A great book for those who feel a bit stuck in their lives and feel they need a bit of a kick to initiate change.

The Little Book of Calm – Paul Wilson (1999, Penguin Books).
A small-format book with one idea for achieving a calm state on each page. Very helpful in times of stress.

Stumbling Through the Undergrowth: A Guide to the Living of Life – Mark Kirwan-Hayhoe (1999, Capall Bann Publishing).
An interesting and personal look at how to achieve a more spiritual lifestyle. The author details his pathway to the unique spiritual beliefs he has built for himself and discusses some of the problems and doubts he has encountered along the way.

The Good Shopping Guide: Ethical Shopping – (ed) Charlotte Mulvey (2002, The Ethical Marketing Group).
The world's first comprehensive ethical reference guide to consumer brands.

Fiction
Lords and Ladies – Terry Pratchett (1989, Corgi).
Terry Pratchett's Witches are fantastic – funny, powerful and full of common sense. Each has definite ideas on what a Witch should be. There is a wealth of knowledge of myth and folklore behind all of Pratchett's books as well as a great story which will keep you hooked and have you in stitches.

The Ordinary Princess – M.M. Kaye (2002, Jane Nissen Books). A classic children's novel finally back in print, this charmingly up-to-date fairy tale has something to teach us all about being down-to-earth and true to yourself.

Organisations
The Samaritans – 08457 90 90 90
P.O. Box 90 90, Stirling, FK8 2SA
www.samaritans.org.uk
Confidential befriending service for people needing to talk about issues such as depression, suicide or self-harm.

Childline – 0800 1111
www.childline.org.uk
Confidential service for children and young people who need to talk to someone about issues such as depression, abuse or self-harm.

MIND – 08457 660 163
15-19 Broadway, London, E15 4BQ
www.mind.org.uk
Confidential service for those needing to talk about or find information on mental health issues including schizophrenia and bipolar disorder.

Relate – 0845 130 40 10
www.relate.org.uk
Confidential advice on relationship issues. Offers face-to-face and telephone counselling by appointment.

Cruse Bereavement Care – 0870 167 1677
www.crusebereavementcare.org
Confidential advice and counselling on dealing with death and grief. Special young person's helpline – 0808 808 1677.

Children of Artemis
BM Artemis, London, WC1N 3XX
www.witchcraft.org
Wicca and Witchcraft organisation with magazine, free online forums and regular talks, conferences and meetings.

Order of Bards, Ovates and Druids
PO Box 1333, Lewes, East Sussex, BN7 1HB
http://druidry.org
Druidry organisation offering information and training.

Pagan Federation
BM Box 7097, London, WC1N 3XX
www.paganfed.org
Organisation for all different Pagan paths, has own magazine and regular talks.

Chapter 2
Responsibility and Ethics

The exercises listed in the previous chapter are not only useful for preparing yourself for Witchcraft, they are ones that experienced Witches should continue doing in order to keep in balance and on the right path. However, once you've spent some time doing them, you should feel more grounded, more in touch with yourself and what you want from life, more in tune with the world and people around you, and happier. All this leads to a greater sense of personal power. On days when you feel on top of the world, you can practically feel the power crackling from your fingertips in a fairy tale kind of way. At this stage it is time to think about personal responsibility and ethics, i.e. how to use your power, when you should use it and when you shouldn't.

Many people like to work to rules for governing the use of personal power, hence such ideas as the Rule of Threefold Return, where whatever you do comes back to you three times (or three times three) as strongly. This same idea can be found in most religions, for example 'do unto others as you would have them do unto you', and concepts of karma (although karma is actually a more subtle idea than merely 'you get what you give'). However, no rules bind you as strongly as ones which you have thought about deeply and voluntarily taken on for yourself in full understanding of all their implications, so I'd just like to take a look at reasons for abiding by certain ethical rules in magical practice.

Ethics

All you need to do is look around you and you will easily see that there is much of what could be termed 'evil' in the world. There is also much stupidity, ignorance, arrogance and selfishness. It is easy to become hardened to this so that you don't notice it any longer, or alternatively feel overwhelmed by it so that you cannot see the good in the world any longer. With today's mass communication and globalisation, we are aware of horrors and unhappiness world-wide more than ever before. It can feel like a hopeless situation which is spiralling out of control more and more quickly, with the world becoming worse and worse on a daily basis. In this climate, what is the point of one individual trying to do good?

The world is large but it is made up of individuals, all of whom can choose to do good or not. One person can make a difference. Try not to be cynical in your dealings with other people or become overwhelmed with the suffering that goes on. All you can do is be responsible for yourself and your behaviour, but this is in itself an awesome task. How do you start and what does it include? Why should you take responsibility for yourself when it may be easier to blame others for your current situation?

Pagans and Witches don't generally believe in a Being specifically responsible for all the evils of the world such as the Christian devil. This is a very significant thing. If there is no supernatural Being responsible for evil, then people are responsible for it. People includes you and me and everything we do every day. The consequences of the smallest action can be far-reaching and should be considered very carefully. There are many social and religious rules telling us why we should do good things rather than bad – our legal system, the emotions guilt and shame, karma, compassion and empathy. Many of these things tell us that the reason we should not do harm is because it will eventually but inevitably rebound on us in some way. However, the simplest law of this kind is the modern Pagan 'harm none'. Simple it may be, but it has profound consequences and you could spend a lifetime meditating on what it may include.

What it doesn't include however, is a reason for harming none – there is no reference to self here, it simply states you should harm none because that is the right thing to do. It is this realisation that makes taking responsibility for yourself both much harder and much more complicated. Although the ethic 'harm none' can be taken from the Wiccan Rede, this is not the first place it is encountered – it is a much older idea than that, the seeds of which can be found in many of the world's religions. One of the first attempts to formalise it into a principle for living by was made by John Stuart Mill in the late 1800s with his argument for the Harm Principle, as he called it. In this argument, potential harm to others was to be the only reason for the state ever to intervene against a sane adult's free will. Obviously, this creates as many questions as it answers, including 'what is included in the definition of harm?' and 'does the attempt at self-harm automatically mean a person is insane and should be restrained?' However, Mill's Harm Principle and the Wiccan-derived 'harm none' can be seen as two sides of the same coin – the same rule stated positively and negatively. One trying to protect the individual's free will and the other laying out the individual's responsibility for the actions carried out under free will.

In any situation, most people try to do the best they can for themselves and their loved ones, but as Witches we should also take responsibility for any further consequences – to the wider community, the strangers we have never met, and to the earth herself. This can lead to some very hard decisions and even lead us to make decisions which are against our own best interest but which benefit the largest number of people. It should also lead us beyond merely doing good because that good will come back to us at some point in this lifetime or another lifetime, and towards doing good as an end in itself, with no expectation of reward. Life is much easier if you think about what you can give rather than what you can get back.

Each of us has to decide what 'harm none' includes, and early on in our path as Witches we should spend a significant amount of time meditating on this point so that we can clearly base our faith and our important decisions on a consistent and thought-through philosophy. It is particularly important that you do not attempt any magic, ritual, spells or healing until you have spent a lot of time considering the ethics of doing so. If you cannot see why this is so important, the following exercise may help you to cover some of the main points although many others will occur to you as you become more experienced as a Witch. We will all encounter our own unique situations where we have to use our judgement about what to do for the best and whether to intervene in either a mundane or magical way. There is no book or teacher to cover every possible situation you may come across, so it is vital to have your own ethical system in place to make such decisions.

In the following exercises there are no right and wrong answers – the questions asked are merely to get you thinking about what you believe and why. As long as you have thought through your beliefs in a consistent and logical manner, no-one should be able to tell you that your beliefs are 'wrong'. It is always useful to have your beliefs challenged, as someone else may have thought of a point which you had not, and defending your beliefs forces you to re-assess why you hold them.

Exercises

• Does 'harm none' include only humans or does it include animal life as well? If so, what consequences might this have for the way you live your life? If not, why not? If you think it applies to animals but in a lesser way than for humans, why is this so and what consequences might it have for your lifestyle?

Does it include plant life, such as trees? Why or why not and what consequences will this have for you? Does it include inanimate objects such as rocks, seas and volcanoes? Again, why or why not and what consequences will this have for the way you live your life?

• What sort of harm is covered by 'harm none'? Is it only physical harm, so that you are prohibited from killing someone or punching them? Does it include inciting other people to harm someone, but not actually becoming involved yourself? Does it include psychological, spiritual or emotional harm, and if so, how do you define these terms? What if you harm someone unintentionally? What if the harm was unintentional but due to your thoughtlessness, carelessness or neglect?

What if you interfere with someone's free will – is this harm? This question is especially relevant for issues around love and relationships, healing and in looking after children. Are there ever any situations where attempting to heal someone could be doing them a harm – for example a terminally ill person, or someone who considers your form of healing evil and would be horrified to know you had used it on them? How far is it justified to restrict a child's free will in order to keep her safe from the unrealised consequences of her own actions or in order to teach her how life works?

Can you ever be 'cruel to be kind'? Might there ever be a justification for doing someone a small harm to prevent a much larger harm to themselves or others – for example smacking a child or shopping someone to the police for a crime they have committed.

What about harm to yourself? Is this covered and how high up the list should it come? As has been mentioned before, self-esteem and self-confidence are very important in being happy and in balance, so hopefully you will not want to harm yourself. If you find yourself in a situation where you are tempted to harm yourself, seek help from a friend or doctor. What about indirect harm to yourself by simply putting yourself and your needs last on the list and thereby exhausting yourself?

These exercises should show that this is a huge subject area with the potential to affect the way you live every part of your life and make every decision in every situation. Of course, you do not have the time to think out all these connected larger questions every time you have to make a decision, which is why you should spend some time thinking about them now and working out your general answers in advance in order to give you a moral framework for making everyday decisions.

It should also be obvious why you should not attempt any kind of magic or healing until you have thought about these things as your answers to these large questions can affect your whole ethical approach to Witchcraft and what you feel it is appropriate to do in a given situation.

Your decisions about your ethical and moral beliefs may surprise you and lead you to make changes to your lifestyle. You may find that your beliefs do not entirely tally with the current laws where you live, or with the general social consensus of the people around you. You may feel led to protest about issues which you didn't feel strongly about before. Remember that all these actions should be performed within the confines of 'harm none' too.

Despite having strong beliefs, you can harm other people by being intolerant of beliefs different to your own; you can harm by being prejudiced; you can harm by breaking the law, whether you agree with it or not; and you can harm by being deliberately offensive to those you disagree with. It is important to uphold your moral beliefs but there is a big difference between being someone who lives by their principles and someone who shoves their beliefs down other people's throats at every opportunity. There are ways of discussing differing beliefs without arguing and this is a beneficial process to all concerned.

One last point – sometimes you may be tempted to go against your principles due to peer pressure, time, convenience or lack of confidence, and sometimes you will give in to this temptation. Don't beat yourself up about it too severely. It's good to think carefully about what led you to give in on this occasion and to try not to do it habitually, but we all have occasional slips – we are only human. Equally, if you see another person acting against their own proclaimed beliefs, don't judge them too harshly – you don't know what pressures have led them to this action.

Responsibility

Once you have thought about the moral and ethical issues involved in life and decided on a moral framework for guiding your actions and decisions, you then have a reason and moral obligation to take responsibility for yourself and your own actions. There is no point accepting the adage 'harm none' and then thinking that you have no control over whether you harm anyone or not. It may be the case in some situations that you do not have control. For example, if an earthquake strikes and kills and injures many people, you did not have control over that and therefore you cannot take responsibility for it happening. But for actions of your own, you do have control and therefore the responsibility for any consequences.

Sometimes, people deny that they have control over their own actions. They may say that it is 'just in their nature' or that they were 'brought up to do that'. It may be harder to control such instinctive reactions as it cannot be denied that some people are more predisposed to certain behaviour than others. Long-ingrained behaviour patterns can be hard to break. However, the behaviour is yours and the control is, ultimately, yours, even if it takes you some time to learn conscious control. If you harm someone because you lash out when you're jealous, you can try to excuse it by saying that you just have a jealous nature, but this is no real excuse.

Exercise

- If you have an instinctive emotional response to something which could lead you to harm someone, such as anger or jealousy, then try this exercise to learn to control yourself.

Firstly, focus on the behaviour rather than the emotion. Learn to dissociate the feeling of being jealous with the behaviour of lashing out, or the feeling of being angry with the behaviour of losing your temper. The emotion and the behaviour are two separate things. Once you have dissociated them, you will be able to stop yourself lashing out or losing your temper.

Secondly, focus on the emotion. Instead of giving in to it, analyse it. What in the situation triggers this feeling? Is it rational? Is it helpful to the situation? Often you find that it is neither rational nor helpful to you. Maybe it reminds you of a previous situation in which this emotion would have been rational and justified. Separate the current situation from the previous one and remind yourself that the two situations are different and therefore call for different responses.

If your emotional reaction is rational and justified in the current situation then think how to deal with it in the most constructive way. If you are constantly in a situation where jealousy is rational and justified then perhaps you are with the wrong partner. If your anger is justified, think how to deal with it to get the best result from the situation. This may mean leaving the situation and not attempting to deal with it until you have calmed down. It may mean releasing your anger on a safe target, for example hitting a pillow or going to a park and shouting as loudly as you can.

Obviously, anger and jealousy are not the only emotions which people try and evade taking responsibility for, but they are common examples. Is there anything that you often try to excuse yourself for by saying that you 'can't help it'? It can be hard to face up to taking responsibility for our actions, but it is worth it, for when we do so we can truly say we are mature, independent and free people. We are then in control of our lives rather than being slaves to our feelings.

It should also be remembered that some people do not take responsibility for the good that they do or the skills they possess. This is usually linked to low self-esteem or a rather extreme sense of modesty. While no-one likes a boaster, taking pride in the good you have done is part of learning to take responsibility for your own life.

Exercise

- Think of your last big achievement. When someone congratulated you on it, did you mutter something about 'anyone could have done it' or something similarly self-derogatory? Have you ever taken for granted a skill or talent you possess by blaming it on your genes, or your parents making you practise it, or just luck? Don't run yourself down! Be proud to take responsibility for your achievements, skills, talents and the consequences of these too.

Wisdom

Many people think of wisdom as something which comes with age, but this is not necessarily the case. Wisdom is something that can be attained at any age, and just because someone is old does not automatically make them wise. I'm not talking about book-learning here, although that can be a vital ingredient of wisdom, but of worldly wisdom or common sense. This is very important as a Witch because many people will consult you for spells or healing or advice and you need to be able to help them as best you can. If you are ignorant or gullible then you will not be able to help people as best you might.

What is wisdom? It is a difficult concept to define – its opposite, foolishness, is very easy to spot, but wisdom is a much quieter quality and can be overlooked or mistaken for shyness, diffidence or reservation. Wisdom isn't an academic skill, nor is it exactly the same as intelligence. It has more to do with maturity, common sense, worldly experience and an acceptance of the way of human hearts and minds.

So how do you attain wisdom? By watching, listening, studying and thinking. When you watch the people around you, you take in how they behave and why, and you can see more clearly the kind of behaviour which is helpful and the kind which is not. Having as much experience as possible of all kinds of human situations, whether you are directly involved as a participant or indirectly involved as an observer, can lead to a great deal of knowledge which can be passed on as advice to those in similar situations. Obviously, none of us can hope to amass comprehensive knowledge about every possible human situation in one lifetime, so this is where thinking, studying and judging comes into it. Some people seem to be wise beyond their years and it is said of them that they 'have a old head on young shoulders'. This may be due to a subconscious recollection of knowledge attained in previous existences, or a particularly empathetic nature, or just a great deal of common sense applied with a good dash of knowledge. Anyone can cultivate the latter skill with some work and application.

Judgement is a word which has been much maligned and confused with the word judgmental. Actually, these words have two different meanings. Making a judgement is vital in order to react to any situation or person, and it involves weighing up the situation and coming to a sensible conclusion based on the evidence in front of you. Being judgmental has the connotation of making prejudiced or hasty judgements on a person or situation. Obviously, being judgmental in this kind of way is not something to be aspired to, but learning to make accurate and sensible judgements is a vital and useful skill, and one that all truly wise people possess.

We all make judgements every day, sometimes on the flimsiest of evidence about the current situation but based on previous knowledge of similar situations – for example, crossing the road is a skill in which we learn to make sensible judgements about the probable behaviour of the traffic based on our previous experience of how traffic behaves. In dealing with other people, we make judgements on whether or not they are reliable based on their past behaviour, or our own past experience in dealing with people. This is where prejudice can creep in. Maybe once when we crossed the road, a red sportscar filled with rowdy young men jumped the red light and almost caused an accident. From then on, you may be warier of red sportscars or young male drivers. This may be justified due to previous experience but will not hold true in all future cases. However, in another example, we may have a friend who always lets us down – she is always late, forgets when we're meeting and cannot be relied upon in a crisis. She offers to help you move house and based on your previous experience of her, you make the judgement that she cannot be relied upon and refuse her offer. We must learn when it is sensible to regard a piece of experience as an isolated incident and when it should be held up as a general pattern for the way the world works. Then we can use our information about the world as useful for making accurate and wise judgements.

This sort of judgement should be used when processing information received via friends, family, the television, radio, newspapers, internet – so that you are not merely a passive and uncritical receiver for every piece of information coming your way, but an active listener and a thinker.

Exercise

• Think about the way you make judgements about the information you receive every day from the world. Are they all sensible, unhurried, made after obtaining all the information and after thinking critically about the source of the information? Or do they tend to be snap judgements made on the basis of instinct? If a friend tells you something, are you more likely to believe it than if you read it in a newspaper? Why? If you see something in a newspaper are you more likely to believe it than if you saw it on the television? Why? If you saw something in a documentary are you more likely to believe it than if you read it on a website? Why? Hopefully the answers to these questions should have made you think about your own judgements and why you make them. You may realise that you trust information if it is written down more than if it is verbal, or vice versa. You may realise that you trust information from a friend (even if they are not an expert on the subject under discussion) more than from a stranger who is an acknowledged expert in the field. This may show you that you are making judgements using your emotions rather than your intelligence.

This exercise is not meant to denigrate the usefulness of instinct. Instinct can be a very useful part of wisdom. Many of us have experienced this when making a very careful decision about something and all logic and sense tells us to go ahead but our instinct is screaming 'stop'! A wise person knows when to listen to instinct and how to tell it apart from nervous qualms or ingrained prejudice. This is a skill which can only be obtained through practise and thoughtful living.

Exercise

- How often do you truly question what you are told? All information which comes at you from the world is coming from someone's perspective. There is no such thing as objective information, it is all filtered through someone else. This need not be a problem as long as you find out exactly what kind of perspective it is coming from and what agenda is being pushed. We are used to this from politicians, so here's an example from the political world: one party tells you there is good news – more money will be spent on healthcare. The opposition party tells you there is bad news – taxes will be rising. Both of these statements may well be part of the same truth, but they are both told to you from a particular perspective, with a particular axe to grind. Other examples may not be so extreme and therefore may not be so easy to spot, but everything should be looked on as suspect until you know where and who the information comes from originally. Usually, you may be able to trust your friend and you know she would not mislead you intentionally, but where has the information she is telling you come from originally?

With every piece of information, whether it be gossip from a friend, a health scare in the press, a virus scare on the internet, reports of a survey on the news, you should ask yourself the following questions: who is telling me this and why? Where did this information originate? Can I trust the source? And most importantly, does it sound likely? Not every piece of information which sounds unlikely is unreliable, but in many cases, if it sounds unlikely or too good to be true then it probably is.

Wise people learn to differentiate between reliable and unreliable information and end up with the reputation of always being 'in the know'. In reality, they have probably been exposed to the same sources of information as everyone else but have merely learned to sift through and find the gold nuggets among the dross. This is a skill that all wise people possess. You will never find a wise person who is gullible and they will usually question everything and withhold judgement until they feel they have all the relevant facts.

Studying can also be a part of wisdom. Many wise people are also very learned in an academic sense, although they may well not possess conventional qualifications. They have realised that the best way to learn about human ideas and thoughts is to experience as many as possible for themselves. They may well do this partly through meeting many people and talking with them, listening to their thoughts and philosophies, but you cannot meet people from other times and places necessarily, so studying written texts is the next best thing. Many cultures around the world and through time have had scholars who wrote their ideas down for posterity and studying these can be invaluable in opening your mind to new ideas and new ways of thinking and expressing yourself. Fiction and even films and television programmes are useful for 'putting yourself in someone else's shoes' and experiencing things which you may not otherwise experience. This leads to being able to understand other people's actions much better and ultimately to being able to see both sides of any argument and appreciate that there is more than one valid point of view to be held about most subjects. In this way, empathy can be learned, even if it is a skill which does not come naturally to you.

Wisdom is essential for a Witch and one of the reasons that some people believe there should be age restrictions on the practice of magic. Although there is no reason why young people cannot be wise and no reason why older people should automatically be so, it does tend to be the case that we accumulate wisdom as we accumulate experience. We should each think carefully about whether we consider ourselves wise enough to practise, or whether we should limit our practice to working on ourselves until we feel we are ready to help others. This is particularly the case when teaching or mentoring others in the ways of Witchcraft – we must be responsible in this and not try to teach until we have sufficient knowledge and experience to truly be able to fulfil this difficult role.

Healing also requires immense wisdom and judgement as there are many cases when people will come to you who require spiritual or emotional healing rather than physical healing. You will need the wisdom and experience to be able to recognise this and then to help them. This can be much more draining and time-consuming than using a healing technique such as aromatherapy or reiki as it may involve listening, empathising and possibly advising as well as supporting the person through their crisis. Ultimately, such healing can be immensely rewarding and can spark off lifelong friendships as you will have undergone a very intense experience with the person you have healed.

Revenge
A lot of people come to Witchcraft or to Witches looking for revenge, but I can't emphasise this strongly enough – revenge is a very bad idea. Whether or not you believe in karma or

Threefold Return or any other ethical system, revenge is not good for you personally because it fixates you on the past instead of helping you move on towards the future. It may well be the case that at times in your life people let you down, betray you and treat you badly. I'm not suggesting you should lie down and be a doormat for these people to walk all over, but that at no time should you forget that you are a decent human being with standards and morals and that you do not need to sink to such levels. If a situation is intolerable or a person is treating you badly, then just walk out the door. You don't need to accept it, you don't need to tolerate it, but you do need to move on with your life. You may find that you need to talk through your experience with a friend or even a counsellor, but generally speaking, your focus should be on the present and the future, not the past. By thinking vengeful thoughts, planning getting your own back, you have anchored the essence of yourself squarely in the painful situation, even though physically you have left.

A good way to move on is to focus on yourself – pamper yourself, make plans, go out and see friends, play your favourite music. Decide how you're going to go out there and get everything that you want and that you deserve to have. That way you'll have had your revenge without even realising because next time you see the person who caused you such pain, you'll be the great new confident and successful person you always wanted to be.

End of Chapter Relaxation

Indulge yourself with a relaxing bath. Really spend time preparing for the treat to come – arrange everything you'll need beforehand and spend some time rearranging the bathroom to be a haven of peace. Remove any clutter that might distract you and choose some favourite bath foam or oils. Tell other people in the house that you'll be in the bathroom for a while and that you don't want to be disturbed by requests to use it, or by your mother on the phone. Shut the curtains and light as many candles in and around the room as is practical and safe. Play some music that you find relaxing and soothing. This is an especially good idea if you cannot guarantee being able to block out background noise – relaxation is very hard if you can hear your kids wrecking the living room or your flatmates clattering around in the kitchen. Fill the bath as high as you can and relax back with your eyes shut. Rather than trying to empty your mind, let your thoughts flow through your head, but don't worry about them. Thoughts of worries and anxieties will inevitably come into your head, but try to imagine the thoughts are like goldfish swimming in a bowl – let them flit around but not settle. In this state you may even find that a solution for a problem comes quite easily. If so, let it come, but don't try to force it.

Eventually, your thoughts will settle and you'll find your mind wandering off on its own bizarre train of thought. Follow it and see where it will take you, but do this idly without active effort. Once the water is cold, you should be feeling nicely relaxed. Make sure you don't immediately shatter the mood when you get out of the bath by putting on the overhead light and opening the door to a rush of cold air. You will have created quite a womb-like feeling in the bathroom and you should gradually emerge making sure that you're well wrapped up. Try to keep the relaxed mood as long as possible – perhaps go straight to bed. You may find you sleep very well but have unusually vivid dreams.

Further Reading
Non-fiction
On Liberty and Other Essays – John Stuart Mill and John Gray (ed) (1998, Oxford Paperbacks).
As mentioned in the chapter, Mill's ideas of harm are still incredibly relevant today, especially to Pagans and Witches.

His essays are well worth reading for anyone thinking out their own philosophy of life.

How Are We To Live?: Ethics in an Age of Self-interest – Peter Singer (1997, Oxford Paperbacks).
A modern philosopher, Singer is interested in moral frameworks for today's world. In this book, he discusses many issues of particular relevance to Witches including the environment and living in a community.

Philosophy: Basic Readings – Nigel Warburton (ed) (1999, Routledge).
A great starting point for anyone interested in the writings of classic philosophers on various issues of current relevance, such as freedom.

Fiction
His Dark Materials Trilogy: Northern Lights / The Subtle Knife / The Amber Spyglass - Philip Pullman (2001, Scholastic Point).
This trilogy of books, set partly in our own universe and partly in subtly different parallel universes, illustrates perfectly how we each have to construct our own moral and ethical frameworks according to the things we encounter. The young people who are the main protagonists in this series are unable to trust any of the adults in their worlds and so have to think about what constitutes good and evil for themselves. You won't be able to put them down!

Chapter 3
Divinity and Deity

Your approach to divinity and deity – gods and goddesses – will affect the way you do magic and what you believe about it, as well as colouring your whole life. The good thing about Witchcraft is that there is no dogma about what you believe on the matter of deity. You can practise Witchcraft and combine it with any, or no beliefs about divinity. However, as with ethics, it is important to work out in advance what you believe so that you can start to learn more about your chosen path and whatever system of magic it may have.

There is much discussion within Witchcraft on the question of whether it can be combined with non-Pagan religions, such as Christianity or Buddhism. In my opinion, Witchcraft can be combined with whatever religious beliefs you like, although the other religion may not be so flexible on the matter, as it is a framework for practising magic rather than a religion with set rules. I don't believe you can combine Wicca with other religions very easily, simply because Wicca is a complete religious system in its own right which believes in a God and Goddess – this would seem to rule out mixing it with a religion which insisted on only one true God. But, people can and do experiment with mixing religions to create new and exciting faiths which are every bit as relevant in today's society as older traditions. After all, religion should be a living phenomenon – if it is not, then it ceases to have meaning and dies. However, do try to make sure your beliefs are complementary and not contradictory or you will end up feeling very confused.

If you meet and speak to other Witches about their beliefs, you will soon find a huge number of variations on people's views of divinity and the sacred, including views traditionally associated with established religions as well as more personal interpretations. Some people believe in gods and goddesses who exist on other planes of existence, others believe that divinity is within us all, and others still that images of gods and goddesses are powerful archetypes we can call on. If you are not sure what you believe, the best way to decide is to read up on other religions and speak to other people (Witch and non-Witch) on their views. As well as being a fascinating study in its own right, you may come across some ideas which really seem to click for you. In order to start you off, here are some of the main distinctions:

Monotheism

This is the belief that there is only one God (or Goddess). It is traditionally associated with the more conventional religions such as Islam, Christianity and Judaism. However, just because you believe in only one deity, it doesn't mean to say that this has to be the Christian God, or that you believe every other religion has it wrong. Many Pagans and Witches believe that all gods are one, and different names and attributes merely aspects of the one 'source' of divinity. Many people believe in this in a vague way without relating it to monotheism – such as a 'force for good' in the universe. Although you may not consciously think of this as believing in a Deity as such, it is a way of believing in a Divine Force. If you think of Divinity as one 'thing' with many faces, names and characteristics, you could relate the Christian belief in one God with three aspects (Father, Son and Holy Spirit), to the typical Pagan belief in a Goddess with three aspects (Maiden, Mother and Crone). The Pagan belief of a male/female duality in divinity can also be accommodated by this view if you think of male and female as two aspects making up one Being which is beyond gender. Mixing pantheons of deities, such as Egyptian or Celtic, is not a problem with this view as all the pantheons are parts of one whole in any case.

Exercise

- Do you use different aspects of gods and goddesses for different prayers and spellworkings? Think hard about whether you believe they are each a separate entity, or whether you believe you are merely calling on different characteristics of the same deity. Neither is right or wrong, but it will help you to gain more effective results if you know exactly who you are calling on and why. When you meet a member of another religion, do you feel a kinship with them because you believe you are both worshipping the same deity, albeit with a different name and in a different way? If so, you may be a monotheist.

Polytheism

Polytheism is the belief in more than one god or goddess. Therefore, in this view rather than seeing each god and goddess as an aspect of the same Being, each is seen as a separate entity and worshipped, prayed to, and called upon in their own right. If you are a polytheist, it will be very important to learn the correct information about each god and goddess and to approach each in the right way and in the right circumstances. Many polytheists choose one particular pantheon which they feel comfortable with and stick to that – there may be problems mixing pantheons if you believe that each God and Goddess is a separate Deity, as you will get overlap in their spheres of interest and their mythologies will not match appropriately with deities from another pantheon.

Polytheism gives you a ready-made system of worship and spellworking as each God and Goddess will have their own character and attributes and you will learn to have an individual relationship with each. There may well be certain times of the year or festival days sacred to each, and certain problems that each can help resolve.

The gender polarity within the divine (belief in a God and Goddess) that is a common belief in Paganism and Witchcraft can be easily accommodated within polytheism, although it doesn't have to be so. Many people believe that we each have masculine and feminine aspects within us, and that we can all call on both the God and Goddess despite our own gender. This can lead to the belief that the God and Goddess are two parts of the same whole, or two aspects of the same whole, personifying different attributes. Therefore, a belief in a God and a Goddess does not automatically have to imply polytheism, but for some people a separate God and Goddess are intrinsic to their view of balance within their faith.

It should be noted that some people confuse the issue of sexuality with gender and therefore feel that gay people cannot be Witches. In my opinion both sexuality and gender are on a sliding scale rather than fixed 'either/or' options, and we all possess characteristics of both to a greater or lesser degree. I feel it is simplistic to think there must be a woman and a man in order to celebrate a God and Goddess – after all, who decides which are masculine and which are feminine attributes, and how does this fit in with sexuality anyway? If you do believe strictly in a male/female Wheel of the Year cycle, try not to see this as promoting a heterosexual way of life over and above any alternatives. With a bit of insight, it can be seen that the God and Goddess are not the stereotypical nuclear family, and that neither their sexuality or gender are as fixed as may at first be thought. The fertility demonstrated by the Wheel of the Year is not only human reproductive fertility but also fertility of the land and creativity of the mind and spirit – ideas, learning, spiritual progression, personal development, joy, and sexual union.

Exercise

• If you are drawn to one particular pantheon and dislike the thought of mixing and matching, you could be a polytheist. Do you call on different deities for different workings and feel you have an individual relationship with each? Do you dislike the thought of there being one Deity and prefer the concept of many deities? Do you believe in a God and a Goddess who are completely separate individuals?

Pantheism

Pantheism is the belief that God is all things i.e. that everything in the universe is divine and that the Divine is the same as every single thing in the universe. This is a very big idea to get your head around and can have certain implications, the main one being that everything is equally sacred and therefore potentially equally valuable, including you and I, and animals and trees and rocks. Some people also find that holding this belief makes worshipping deities feel a bit silly, as in some ways you are actually worshipping yourself! Therefore, pantheists may talk in terms of respecting, honouring, or acknowledging gods and goddesses (as aspects of the divine) rather than actually worshipping them. The idea that all gods are one fits in well with pantheism as with monotheism, as well as the idea of gods and goddesses as aspects of the all-pervading Divine. Pantheists may also see deities as actual entities who are part of the divine universe, or as helpful archetypes to aid the release of the individual's inner deity.

Some pantheists may believe that living creatures have more of the divine inside them and therefore value a person more highly than a rock or they may believe that all things have equal divinity. Pantheism can be one reason why a person believes in animal rights issues, vegetarianism or environmental issues.

Exercise

• If you believe in your inner God or Goddess, you may be a pantheist. If you are attracted towards the concept of Gaia, Lovelock's theory of a living planet, this would fit in well with pantheistic ideas of the equal divinity of everything in the universe, and could be leading you towards animism – the belief that everything has consciousness. Do you see that little spark of divine power in all things? Do you find it hard to think of deity as actual gods and goddesses and prefer the idea of power being equally in everything? Do you believe in divinity as a force, whether for good, evil or neutral, that surrounds and penetrates us all?

Atheism

Many people may wonder how you could be a Witch and an atheist, but a belief in a deity is not a prerequisite for practising Witchcraft. Being an atheist doesn't necessarily mean that a person has no spiritual or moral beliefs. As I have said before, I believe that Witchcraft is a system for practising magic and not a religion in its own right, therefore it can be practised by people with all sorts of different religious beliefs and those with none. I still believe that Witches need a rigorous ethical and moral system before practising magic, but the type which I outlined previously does not depend on belief in any deity or afterlife, merely a belief in doing what is right in any situation.

Atheism is much more varied than many people realise – it does not have to preclude the belief in an afterlife or a soul. In fact, you may even be an atheist yourself without realising it – you can still believe in magic and in the awesome power of creativity in the universe, just not in a god or goddess.

Exercise

- Do you believe the world as it is today was created by physical forces such as evolution with no input from a supernatural being? Do you believe that spirits of all varieties are in fact just other species that we know little about, rather than deities? Do you believe you control your own destiny rather being part of a grand plan? Do you believe that the whole universe is a giant magical accident rather than designed? Do you believe that you have a soul but that it evolved rather than being created by a deity? Think carefully about these questions and you will see that belief in a deity is not necessary for a spiritual life.

If you wish to explore this issue further, Humanism is a growing approach to life which encompasses people with many different atheist and agnostic approaches to life but who still believe passionately in working within an ethical and moral framework – their approach relies on the predominance of human nature and experience and emphasises human social responsibility.

Immanence and Transcendence

Immanence and transcendence are two different approaches to spirituality. Basically, immanence is the belief that divinity is within the person, while transcendence locates divinity outside the person as something higher to be striven for. Neither belief is right or wrong, but which you believe can have an effect on how you approach magic and mundane life. It can also effect which religious ideas may or may not blend well.

If you feel that divinity is within you, then everything you are is divine. This is a common belief within Paganism where the earth, the body and the sensual appetites are seen as sacred as well as the intellectual and spiritual aspects of a person. However, if divinity is something separate from ourselves, something higher, something purer, then it is often associated with 'higher' pursuits, such as learning and prayer – pursuits seen as 'lower' such as eating and sex are seen as something which divides us from divinity and which should be scorned. Transcendence is often the basis for the belief that fasting and celibacy purify a person and make them more holy.

This is probably putting the matter very simplistically, but it can have great repercussions for how you practise magic – if you are striving to become your higher self, you may well make very different preparations and use a very different method to achieve your ends than if you believe there is no dichotomy between higher and lower self.

Your beliefs on this matter may well influence how you see deity as well – if you believe deity is immanent, then it is part of you and of everyone else too. It would be difficult to make this compatible with the belief that gods and goddesses have a flesh-and-blood existence on another plane. However, if you believe that the gods and goddesses are higher beings which we can try to be more like, then it could be hard to be a pantheist and see divinity within everything in the universe.

Sometimes our instinct is to believe in two mutually incompatible concepts, and it is surprisingly easy not to notice when we are doing this until someone else points it out. It is important to test your own beliefs for inconsistencies and incompatibilities. When you have been convinced that a concept is true for many years and have been basing an important part of your life on this assumption, it can be devastating to have the rug pulled out from under your feet by a casual remark made by a stranger. Far better to think things out at the very beginning of the practise of your faith and to constantly test them, so that you always know where you are and what you think. People can be very cruel (often unintentionally) in pointing out other people's errors.

There are tendencies for extremism in both forms of belief. Just because you believe that divinity is within you, it doesn't mean that indulging excessively in every sensual pleasure is necessarily a divine activity. I'm sure we can all see the difference between sipping a glass of wine while appreciating its flavour, and drinking ten pints of lager in order to get plastered. Despite the concept of immanence suggesting that all you do is divine automatically, if you do things without thought then they are no more divine than a pint of custard! It is certainly true that eating, drinking, and having sex can be sacred activities when they are done mindfully and with spiritual intention (for example as part of a ritual, or in order to honour the earth or season). But then, all everyday activities can be sacred if done with this mindset.

Exercíse

- See if you can live one whole day doing everything with sacred intent. Concentrate on finding the magic and wonder in everything you do, from cleaning your teeth, cooking the dinner, going to work, doing your homework, mowing the lawn, to going to bed again in the evening.

You will soon see that being part of the Divine doesn't necessarily mean that everything you do is sacred or divine all the time. Putting the right intent into things takes effort, concentration, energy – and practise! If we could all manage it all the time we'd be joys to live with, always happy, and constantly plugged in to that wonderful feeling of 'oneness' and connectedness with the universe.

No-one can keep it up all the time, but if you just think about it occasionally and try to find the sacredness in one activity every day then that is an excellent start and should make you feel much better within yourself.

The temptation with the belief in transcendence is to withdraw too much from the world. Obviously, if you are a nun or a monk, then this is the whole idea, but in general Witches are not nuns or monks and are actually intending to live in the world and give something back to it on a community level. I'm sure you've all noticed how much easier it is to be in tune with the universe and with yourself when you're on holiday somewhere peaceful and you don't have to argue over whose turn it is to do the cooking or the washing up, and the everyday world of work, school, television and bills is far behind you. This is an example of your higher self and shows you how you could be without mundane distractions.

However, unless you truly are going to withdraw from the world in some way, we all have to find a way to square the distractions of the workaday world with the quest for transcendence.

Exercise

    • Spend a day making a chart – every activity you do mark on it how much it distracts you from your higher self on a scale of one to ten, and how much it really matters in the grand scheme of things, again rated on a scale of one to ten. Hopefully by the end of the day you should be seeing a pattern – that things distract you far more than they should for the amount they actually matter in life. This is something we probably all do – let things get to us far more than they should. This is because these things don't happen in isolation, it is one thing after another after another, and inevitably it will get to breaking point. This is the point where you inexplicably lose your temper over something really small and your partner, friends, family or kids all stare at you open-mouthed while you blush and know that you're over-reacting and yet can't seem to stop yourself.

If this seems familiar, try the small trick of reminding yourself how little each event matters as and when it occurs. Also, try to recognise the build-up of the big explosion, and remove yourself to small haven of peace such as a bathroom or bedroom before it happens. Be kind to yourself, transcendence is hard.

A common failing which can happen with both types of belief is – making some progress and then becoming unbearably holier-than-thou. Always remember that it is not a sign of great spiritual awakening to be smug and annoy your friends and family! You will also not be in great demand for advice, help and healing if you are this far out of step with people and their needs. It should always be borne in mind that your spirituality is not just for your benefit – it is to help others and ultimately make the world a better place.

Concepts of Deity

There are a great many ways of seeing the divine, all of which are equally valid. Another one to consider is how you think of your gods and goddesses. Do you believe they are flesh and blood beings like ourselves, but of another, higher, species or from another world? Do you believe they are real beings but made of spirit or ether rather than of physical bodies? Do you think they have been formed, shaped and given power by human belief over the years? Or do you believe they are archetypes for stimulating power from our own subconscious? All these views are held by Witches and provoke further, and different, questions.

If you believe the gods and goddesses have physical bodies, then where do they come from and where do they live? How do they communicate with us and how do we know their intentions are good? How do we know they are 'higher' than us at all? They could merely be different. What sort of power do they have and how can we request they use it to help us? There is very little evidence to answer these questions definitively and for many people this is a matter of faith and trust. There could also be other beings which fit into this category of flesh and blood creatures, such as aliens, angels, fairies and elemental beings. Some people believe in them and some people don't. Some people claim to have met such creatures and some people still wouldn't believe in them even if they did meet one. This is a matter for each person to decide, bearing in mind your instincts, experience, common sense and your personal requirement for hard evidence.

Probably a more common belief is that deities are real but spiritual beings. Once again, the questions need to be asked: where do they live and how, how do they interact with us and how can we become aware of them? How do we know their intentions are honourable and how can we tell deities apart from any bad or mischievous spirits there might also be out there, trying to harm us? It is easier to see how to incorporate spiritual beings in spells and rituals – invoking is a fairly common way of attempting to use the power of a spiritual being in our own spells and workings. Many people may feel they have a personal relationship with a god or goddess as a spiritual presence, or some other form of spirit such as an animal guide, the spirit of a dead relative or some form of guardian spirit. This is a very intuitive way of seeing the gods.

A third way of viewing deities is as anthropomorphic concepts – that mankind has invented the gods as person-shaped representations of natural occurrences in order to try and explain these occurrences and then control them, such as a

God of Thunder or Rain. Even if this is so, the worship and belief of generations of people could well have given such gods quite a resonance within us and therefore power of their own outside of our expectations. Just because something is 'made up' doesn't mean it has no power.

Another way of looking at deities is as aids to the subconscious, perhaps in the form of archetypal images. This is quite different to the first two viewpoints (and more like the third) as it effectively denies that gods and goddesses are objectively real beings and instead believes that they are manifestations of parts of our own psyches. This is not to deny them power or status though - as we have already seen, many people believe that we all have divine aspects within ourselves and this viewpoint fits well with that belief. The psychologist Jung believed that our subconscious is a very powerful tool, able to exert its will on the world given the right stimulus. This is the basis of such practices as visualisation and hypnosis – appealing to the very deepest parts of our brain in order to achieve the results we require. Jung suggested that one way of doing this was the use of archetypal images – ideas and symbols which are very old and which suggest a particular idea to our subconscious while bypassing the conscious part of our brain which might misinterpret or pooh-pooh the idea. Therefore, seeing gods and goddesses as archetypal images is to believe them very powerful indeed, although it does require a slightly different way of harnessing that power in workings.

End of Chapter Relaxation

This reward is based on earthly pleasures but will still hopefully appeal to those of you who prefer transcendence to immanence! Prepare, or get someone else to prepare for you, your favourite meal. Try and make it with fresh, organic ingredients and with sacred intent. Also prepare a favourite drink, but try to make it something fairly pure, such as spring water, fresh fruit juice, or wine – as opposed to Tizer or squashes. Sit down at a table to eat the meal – not in front of the television or while on the phone – and give the meal your full attention. Savour each mouthful and really taste each flavour, taking your time over each and every bite. Does this food taste better than the usual rushed, re-heated supermarket meal? Can you see how this simple idea can be thought of as sacred? Does the pleasure you get from the meal stay with you for longer than usual?

Furthen Reading

Non-fiction
Dictionary of Gods, Goddesses, Devils and Demons – Manfred Lurker (1987, Routledge).
A huge book listing deities from many cultures and religions both current and ancient. Not much information given on each one, but will give you a starting point for further research.

Gaia: A New Look at Life on Earth – James Lovelock (2000, Oxford Paperbacks).
An updated version of Lovelock's classic living earth theory.

Introducing Jung – Maggie Hyde (1999, Icon Books).
A simple, but thorough introduction to the psychological and spiritual aspects of Jung's work.

Fiction
Small Gods – Terry Pratchett (1993, Corgi Books).
Another great book by Pratchett combining his great breadth of knowledge with humour and an absorbing story on the theme of divinity.

The Hitchhiker's Guide to the Galaxy – Douglas Adams (1988, Pan).
A classic start to the Hitchhikers series of books, Adams has his own definite views on deity in these books which can be useful for making us question our own preconceived notions. It is also a hilariously funny and fiendishly clever read.

Contacts
British Humanist Association, 47 Theobalds Road, London, WC1X 8SP.
www.humanism.org.uk

Chapter 4

Magic and Spells

You may think that I've taken an inordinately long time to reach this subject – some people seem to think that it is the main point of being Witch. However, I think it is merely one of the parts of being a Witch and not the most important one by a long chalk. I also think that it is entirely right that people should take a long time being trained or training themselves before ever attempting a spell. The first spells attempted then should be very simple ones and for yourself. Only after you have experienced the practical workings of magic and how the results work should you try to do magic for anyone else.

If you have worked through the chapter on ethics, this should be obvious, but just in case: never do a spell for someone without their explicit knowledge and permission. It would be very unethical and possibly dangerous because it attempts to limit their free will. They could be violently opposed to all forms of magic, which could easily unbalance the intent of a spell from you. It could be that you are not in full possession of all the facts, so that your spell would then be completely inappropriate for the circumstances. If you would like to do a spell for someone and you are not sure of their reaction to you being a Witch, you could break it down for them and say something like 'I'd like to send you some healing' or even that you'll pray for them – a prayer does not have to be a Christian prayer to the Christian God but can simply be an intercession with a deity, of whatever religion.

There are two important points to discuss regarding magic – firstly, what is it? And secondly, when should you use it? With both of these questions, the opposite question immediately needs answering in order to answer the main one – what isn't magic? And, when shouldn't you use it?

Magic isn't like in the movies – I cannot stress this enough. Due to media exposure of magic and Witchcraft on television and in books and films such as Harry Potter, Charmed, Buffy, Sabrina and The Craft, Witchcraft is more in the news than ever before. This is a good thing as it opens people's eyes to different possibilities, and they are enjoyable to watch and read. However, just as we do not expect a real-life Witch to have green skin and a wart on her nose as portrayed in fairy tales, we should also not expect fictional portrayals of magic to be realistic. Some films and books may have researched Wicca and modelled their rituals and wording on published sources, but they are entertainment media, not documentaries and we should not be expecting factual displays of magic from such sources. So, drop all illusions of changing eye colour, freezing time or fighting demons. Witchcraft is a down to earth, common sense practice concerned with honouring the earth and giving back to the community. This may make it seem less glamorous than on the television – and this is true. Being a Witch is not glamorous, it is hard work, about being disciplined and learning wisdom. However, if you work hard at it, I guarantee you will get more reward and satisfaction out of it than the people on the telly ever seem to.

So that covers what magic is not. Now when not to use it. Magic shouldn't be the first and only thing you try in order to resolve a situation. For example, if you want a new job, by all means do a spell to help your confidence in interviews or to attract the right advert your way, but you'll never get a job if you don't polish up your mundane skills such as CV writing and filling in applications. Equally, other people may ask you to help them with magic, when what is actually needed is action in the mundane world. For example, if someone is worried about their health because they've suddenly lost a lost of weight without trying to, and they come to you for a magical solution – in this circumstance your knowledge should tell you that this can be a symptom of some very serious illnesses, and what is actually required of you is to support the person through the ordeal of going to the doctor as soon as possible and preparing for the possibility of bad news, at the same time as staying positive for a less serious outcome. This kind of situation is tricky to negotiate - the person who has come to you probably knows deep down what they should do but has come to you instead hoping for a quick fix or unconsciously needing emotional support. You have to be strong enough, experienced enough and tactful enough to explain what is really needed and to refuse any magical interference, apart from lending strength, until a diagnosis is made. It is a clear situation when you should not use magic.

There may be other situations in which a combination of magic and mundane action is required. For example in the case of a child telling you about bullying at school. Firstly, you should not do any magic for, or on, an underage person without the knowledge and consent both of the young person and a parent. If you question this, think how you would feel if someone baptised your child into another faith without your knowledge or permission. You may feel the two situations are not analogous but many people who object to Witchcraft for some reason may not agree. Secondly, this situation can be helped by practical action combined with magic, but not necessarily by magic alone. It will help the person being bullied just to know they can talk to you about the situation. The worst thing about being bullied is the isolation it imposes on you – you are singled out and deliberately separated from the crowd. Sometimes people you thought were your friends will also desert you, from fear of becoming the next victims themselves. The bullies depend on the loneliness and despair that this causes in their victims which makes it harder to speak out. When a bullied person first speaks to someone else about the situation they have taken a huge first step in conquering the problem. In purely practical terms, you can then help the person to speak to their parents or the teachers at school – you can be an adult advocate who may be more articulate and whose word may carry more weight with other adults (sad but often true).

On a spiritual level, you can try to help build up the bullied person's self-esteem which may have been completely shattered by the bullying. Sometimes succeeding in giving a person their confidence back is enough to stop the bullying, as bullies are cowards and will only pick on easy targets, not strong ones. On a magical level, you can do spells to aid a positive outcome to the situation and to help build strength and confidence in the bullied person. You could also teach them some simple self-help methods such as meditation for relaxation and visualisation for confidence. As has been noted before, spells for revenge or that the bullies 'get what they deserve' are not a good idea, as they focus your energy on the current situation and not the positive outcome which you require. It is also unethical as you are probably not in full possession of the facts. Bullies are usually cowards and are often people with a lot of problems themselves – wishing further problems on them will not help either the bully or the victim.

Often, the real magic you can perform is in saying the right thing or presenting it in a way which makes sense to the person needing help. This may sound simple but is vitally important and takes great insight, intuition, skill, wisdom and practise! Sometimes a person will outline their problem or situation but will not emphasise the part that is really causing concern – maybe they are not even aware themselves of the part that is of greatest concern – and you will need the skill to home in on the part that needs healing greatest and concentrate your efforts there first. It may be that comfort or reassurance is required, or maybe practical suggestions and help. Maybe the person is trying to tell you something they are ashamed of or not really sure they want to share – such as an eating disorder. The best spell you can do in these cases is to respond in the most helpful way for the individual you are trying to help.

Maybe many people have tried to help them before – your magical skills should enable you to outline a solution which really rings a bell with the person and inspires them to be able to carry out the course of action recommended. In short, the real magic is in empowering the person to be able to cope themselves, to wake their own power. If you can do this, you have given a great gift, as the person will then not need to come to you for help with future problems – you will have given them the skills to cope for themselves.

Magic is not something to be used in trivial situations and a great many Witches find they do not actually do spells that often, nor need to. I will not be giving lists of spells and how to do them in this book as people do spells and magic in many different ways and it is pointless using a spell written by someone else for a completely different situation. Likewise collecting spells – this is pointless as each spell should be created by its caster for a particular situation and outcome, and not collected like stamps in a book. I believe that there is no point casting a spell until you are able to create one yourself – if you need to be given instructions then you aren't ready to do it.

Magic should mean something to you personally – it should be something you feel, and the contents of a spell and how to cast it should be something which comes to you intuitively with each different situation. Sometimes you may use one method – candle magic for example, and on another use herbs. 'Writing' a spell may well not be really accurate as a spell is not just a piece of rhyming poetry declaimed in ritual settings, it is all about your power and your intent focused on your desired outcome. You may never use any equipment at all, but only visualisation – or you may infuse a lovingly-cooked meal with healing intent. This is very common and even people who do not believe in magic will use this kind of magic on a sick child – how many of us remember our own mothers or fathers making us a special meal when we were ill, or 'kissing it better' when we had hurt ourselves. Do you also remember how well it worked? The pure intent of parental love is hard to beat in a spell.

So, if people who don't actually believe in magic sometimes use it, then what is magic? And when should it be used? The definition of magic which I work to is that it is projecting my will into the universe i.e. it is the art of effecting the course of reality according to what I want to happen. This definition encompasses many different views of where the power for this actually comes from. It could be from within yourself, either channelled from elsewhere or originating inside you. Or it could come from outside yourself, either from the universe or a god or goddess. Neither of these views is either right or wrong, they are just different beliefs and you will have to decide which one you find suits you best. Whichever view you eventually take on board, you as an individual are very important in focusing and directing the magic to where you wish it to work. If you are unable to concentrate and focus, the power could rush off in all directions and potentially cause harm, or at the very least mean your spell will not work.

All methods of magic and spells are different ways of focusing our intent. Some ways are intended to magnify our intent (like using a lens to focus it more sharply) by adding natural power to our own – for example, timing spells to appropriate times of the moon or of the year. The whole point of all spells though is they have to mean something to you – there is no use reading up on a complicated system of symbolism to use on spellwork if the symbols seem wrong or unnatural to you.

It is your intent and power you are using, so it must be personal to you. This does not mean you can't use a pre-published spell, as long as seems right to you.

Protection

People disagree hugely on what protection is necessary before attempting any kind of working. Therefore, once again, this is an issue to decide for yourself before you start to practise. How likely you are to need protection depends entirely on your view of the world and the entities within it – who do you think will need protection from? If you believe in spiritual beings, fairies, angels, demons, disembodied human spirits, or any other form of life apart from human then it will have crossed your mind that some of these beings may not be well-disposed towards humans. Some may be merely neutral towards humans but others may be mischievous or actively malevolent. You may believe they could attack you at any time or only under certain circumstances when you make yourself vulnerable such as in meditation or astral travel. Some people like to wear protective charms or amulets all the time as a precaution, some people protect their homes with spells such as salt on all thresholds to the outside, and some people do a protection ritual before doing any working such as casting a circle or visualising a shield of white light around themselves.

If you do not believe in other entities or you believe that they cannot or would not harm you, then that leaves other humans to protect yourself from. It should be against any Witch's ethical code to attack another person either magically or physically, but unfortunately there are always unscrupulous people out there who act selfishly or thoughtlessly. There are also people who are not Witches and who may unconsciously attack another person magically. We've all encountered people like this, who make us feel weak and drained when in their company. Young children are especially good at sending out waves of concentrated hatred when frustrated as they have not yet learned to discipline their emotions. However, such 'attacks' should not be too worrying – people who unconsciously send out negative energy and those too unscrupulous to subscribe to a proper ethical framework are usually not powerful or focused enough to actually do any harm, whatever they may say or intend. Remember that you, as a disciplined and experienced Witch, will always be more powerful than them and can therefore repel any negative energy sent your way, unless you give it power yourself by believing in its harm. By all means give yourself added strength by using whatever charms, amulets, protection spells and rituals make you feel safe, but at the end of the day, it is your power, your discipline and strong sense of self which keeps you safe.

Grounding is a different form of protection and one which is very useful for meditation purposes. It is just a simple technique for making sure you do not get too engrossed in your practise and forget to come back to the real world. Once you really get the hang of meditation and visualisation it can be easy to end up feeling really 'spacey' and out of it, and you can find that afterwards your body does not feel like yours for a while. To prevent this kind of feeling, always ground yourself by imaging a tether of some sort tying you securely to the ground. That way the tether will always tug you back if you go too far or for too long or if something frightens you. And always have something small to eat and drink after meditating – this helps to bring you back fully to your body and its sensations and helps you disassociate from your meditative experiences.

Meditation

Meditation is an excellent practice to cultivate as it is great for relaxation, centring, focusing and getting to know yourself. There are many different forms of meditation and some are associated with a particular form of religion such as Buddhism, or a particular school of thought such as Transcendental Meditation. There are many different techniques for meditating depending on what you are trying to achieve. You can try to completely empty your mind in order to free yourself from distractions, or you can try to fill it with one particular image such as a candle flame, for the same purpose. However, until you are very practised, I would suggest a slightly simpler method.

Find a comfortable position. This need not be a classic meditation position such as the lotus position (and indeed for most you, definitely will not be as such positions require a lot of practise and flexibility in order to be anything approaching comfortable) and may well be lying down. Make sure you are not hungry, thirsty, hot, cold or too full from a meal. This is very important as nothing is more likely to distract you from meditating than physical discomfort of some sort. Don't feel that you have to hold your body rigidly immobile throughout. The key is to relax, but if you get cramp or an itch, sort it out without fuss and go back to your practise. If you fall asleep, as is very common, it doesn't matter – it just means you have at least mastered the art of relaxation! Try not to put a lot of pressure on yourself to 'succeed' with some heavy purpose the very first time you try meditation and equally, don't try to meditate for an hour the first time – just aim at a couple of minutes and build it up as your confidence and ability grows.

You may find silence helpful or you may be one of those people who find silence oppressive. It may be that because of other occupants of your house, there is never silence anyway. In which case, block out background noise which is likely to disturb you with some soothing and quietly-played music or natural sounds like ocean waves or birdsong. Shut out animals and children – both are very good at sensing exactly when you least want to be disturbed and then disturbing you!

Exercise

- You might want to record this onto a tape to listen to: shut your eyes and take several deep breaths in and out. Remind yourself that in your room, in your house you are completely safe. As you breath out, consciously relax your muscles, starting with your forehead and lower jaw, moving down to your shoulders and hands, your stomach and finally your knees and feet. While you do this, imagine a rope of some sort and whatever colour you want tied to your waist and attaching you securely to the floor. This rope grounds you and protects you from any bad thoughts you may have. While in the meditative state, you are completely safe.

Many thoughts will come into your mind. Just let them – neither pursue them nor try to ignore them. Don't let any of them make you re-tense your muscles. Practise letting the thoughts swim around in your mind without reacting to them – as if they were someone else's. Sometimes, the thoughts will clear and you will enter a period of thinking of nothing. Sometimes one particular thought will dominate and a solution or new idea connected to it will emerge in your mind. Sometimes you may hear a voice speaking in your mind or see some sort of a vision or get a sense of particular well-being. Just let whatever comes happen. You are completely safe. If you ever feel uneasy while meditating, just open your eyes and leave the state. When you are ready to come back to normal life, try and do so gradually – firstly move your toes, then your fingers and neck. Finally, open your eyes. Despite your anchoring rope you may feel a little 'spacey' to start with so have a glass of water and a biscuit to bring yourself back down to earth again. If you encountered anything interesting, write it down as soon as possible afterwards as the memory may fade.

This form of meditation is a very basic one which can be practised purely for relaxation or taken further for workings with specific intent. It is a good idea to practise the basic version for a while before trying to take it further. It will come more naturally to some people than others, just as any other skill but don't worry if you find it hard. Putting pressure on yourself will just make it less likely that you'll be able to relax and will make the whole thing harder. Some people find different times of the day suit them better or different rooms of the house.

Visualisation

Visualisation is a method of achieving the outcome you desire by imagining it happening in detail. This may sound silly but it really works! How many times have you wanted something to happen but then immediately presumed it wouldn't? Many people have a self-defeating mindset which automatically assumes they will not be able to do the thing they really want to. They have stopped themselves from achieving what they want with a self-fulfilling prophecy. Some people may get further and set out to achieve the goal they desire, but then fail. They then tell themselves 'see, I knew I couldn't do it'. Once again they have set themselves up for failure. Visualisation is using the opposite idea, in which we set ourselves up for success.

Every thought and intent we have exists somewhere in the universe – we may not be able to see it, but it is there. If you constantly dwell on a negative outcome to something, you create a whole cloud of negativity in which the undesired outcome 'happens'. Everything in the universe is connected. We can see evidence of that every day in the way we all affect each other's actions. The weather and general environment affect us, someone else's bad mood can be infectious, just as someone else's laughter can be. Therefore, why is it so hard to believe that dwelling on bad things can make them more likely to happen? Never underestimate the power of positive thinking. Think of those people who always seem to be optimistic no matter what happens – in the end, things seem to turn out well for them. They expect and imagine a good outcome, and that is what they are more likely to get.

Visualisation takes this one step further, so that while in a meditative state you actually construct in detail a picture of your desired outcome. You make it so realistic in your mind, with sound, texture, and colour that it is practically real already. You focus the whole power of your intent into willing this outcome to happen. You can use this technique to send healing to someone by constructing an image of them becoming well. You can imagine getting the new job you want, or passing the exam. Or you can use it for less specific things such as making a decision or attempting to see an animal spirit guide. All you need to do is to set up the right picture in your mind and focus your intent on what you want to happen. This may sound simplistic but it is a very powerful method and should not be used for unethical ends. Always remember to be careful what you wish for – imagining yourself as a millionaire may seem like a good idea, but the universe has a way of playing tricks on people and unless you can be sure that you have left no detail out in specifying exactly where the money comes from, leave well alone. There is a famous story about a person wishing for wealth who gained it only when a close and much-loved family member died and bequeathed it in their will. So, although there is nothing wrong with doing spells for your own gain, be careful that no-one could be harmed by the consequences and beware of the cosmic trickster!

Some people may wonder how visualisation can possibly work, saying that it is 'only imagining things'. But if you stop to think about it, we all take quite for granted the fact that our mind controls many things in the physical world – we think about opening a door and the power of our mind alone makes our hand and arm move to obey the command. It took us quite a while as babies and children to master the fine control needed for everyday movements such as writing, but now we don't even think about it when we want our bodies to move. This is a fine example of the power of the mind to control aspects of the physical world and the fact that it takes practise to become skilled at the technique. The power of the placebo effect in healing is also well documented, whereby if a person believes they are receiving a cure, they will be cured. Again, this shows the power of the mind to influence physical events and lays the basis for the way visualisation works.

Exercise

• Usually you will think up your own visualisations, in order to make them more relevant to you, but to start with it can be helpful to use ones already written. The following example is intended to help make a decision:

Lie down and breathe deeply, tense each muscle in your body and then deliberately release each one. Let all heaviness and tension go, shut your eyes and feel your body float. Tune into the element of air and let it come to you and fill you with its properties of freedom, lightness and wisdom. Feel yourself soaring into the sky, first rising with the currents of heat from your house and then out into the open sky. Feel the rushing of the wind in your face and the cold of the air as you fly higher. The air buoys you up and you laugh out loud at the sheer joy of flying unfettered above the earth. Down below you can see towns and fields but that life feels very distant now. Up here, you are able to see through all that to what really matters. Down below you can see the world laid out as if it is a map. Up ahead of you is a fork in road with a number of different turnings. You realise these are different consequences of your decision. From this high in the air, you can see all the options clearly and you can follow each one from this safe distance in the air. The solution now becomes clear. The path you should take seems obvious to you now. Things that were worrying you attain their proper perspective and you are able to let go of trivial worries and problems that are not within your power to solve. The higher you fly, the more clear things become. The fresh, chill wind rushes past you, taking negativity away and replenishing your positive energy. You feel sober, wise and assured as you realise that you are flying high over your own house again. When you feel ready, you swoop gracefully down to land back where you started, but with the abilities and insights you have gained from your flight intact.

Visualisation can be a tricky skill to master. It takes practise and it takes focus and discipline. But don't despair if you can't do it immediately – if you wanted to learn to play the piano you wouldn't expect to able to sit down in front of it first time and play Beethoven's Moonlight Sonata! In the same way, meditation and visualisation take time and practise, especially since they are opposite to the type of skills normally required of us in the everyday world. Many people find it hard to relax their bodies and quiet their minds, and most people will at least sometimes find it hard to stop everyday issues crowding into their mind. If you lie down to meditate or visualise and it just isn't working, don't get frustrated, simply try to get the most out of a short period of relaxation that you can, and then try again another day. The same is true if it is hard for you to find the time to meditate regularly or for long periods. Just do what you can manage and don't think that just because you haven't meditated for a week or a month that you might as well give up. You may make slower progress, but every little helps and it's worth doing it once a month rather than not at all.

This is an area of your practise that your children can benefit from too – try to build a 'quiet time' into their day from an early age, perhaps after a meal when they may be more inclined to be quiet anyway. Play some soothing music and sit down comfortably together, perhaps cuddling up or stroking your child's back. Get them used to the idea of being calm and quiet regularly for short spaces of time. For older children, you could ask them to shut their eyes and think up a pretend story or imagine they are doing something wonderful that they've always wanted to do. Afterwards they could write down or draw what they imagined and you talk about it together – you may be surprised at how vivid their thoughts can be! It is a valuable twofold skill they are learning: to quiet their minds, and to stimulate their imaginations. Anecdotal evidence of doing such exercises for children in schools has shown them very successful.

Equipment

You may have noticed that the methods I have outlined do not require any form of equipment or props. They also do not require a formal ritual or rite, or any set words or poetry. This does not mean that such things cannot be useful in their place if you find them helpful, but I believe that all Witches should be able to tap into their power without any kind of prop or ritual. The equipment and formal rites should be there to help you, or for a very special occasion.

There are two kinds of people in the world – those who like fancy dress parties and those who don't – in the same way, people are split into those who find formal ritual helpful for building atmosphere and power and those who find it distracting for building atmosphere and power. You should know the kind of person you are, but if you don't, here's a simple test – do you enjoy building up an altar with all the 'right' things on it, buying candles and athames and having special robes to perform magic in? Do you enjoy the theatricality and drama of writing or learning special words for a midnight robed ceremony? If so, you are someone who finds the structure and framework of having recipes and instructions to follow reassuring and helpful to calling up your power, and may find it more comfortable to work using equipment and rituals.

If you feel that buying special items is pointless, have never felt the urge to construct an altar, you perform spells in your kitchen wearing an apron, and find set ritual positively off-putting, then you are the sort of person who will be happiest using pure intent alone for magic. In this case, spend time exploring your meditation and visualisation skills. If you get really good, you will find that you can capture some of the correct state wherever you are and whatever you're doing. You'll find that you can focus your will and intent much more easily and you may never even say a word out loud.

If you enjoy using equipment and rituals, then a word of warning – don't become too reliant on any one item. Always remember that the power should come from or through you and the piece of equipment is merely a prop to aid you. Don't feel that you have to go out and buy a whole load of stuff, and don't worry that you haven't bought the 'right' stuff or that you haven't arranged it in the 'right' way. There are many different opinions on the right way of doing things and if you try to listen to them all you will merely get confused and frustrated. By all means read several different opinions on the subject, but at the end of the day have the confidence and skill to listen to your own intuition about what is right for you, and then do it that way. And stick to it no matter what anyone else might say.

The world is full of people glad to tell you that you're doing it wrong. However, the whole point is for it to be meaningful and right for you and you alone. For example, in any Wiccan primer you will find lists of correspondences – colours, moon phases, astrological signs, crystals. It's always worth reading up on these, as there's no point reinventing the wheel if the ready-made lists are meaningful to you, but if you find one doesn't work for you, change it! If you want to do a candle magic spell to help you pass an exam, you may well be looking for colours that will correspond to wisdom, success and confidence. I would use pale blue for wisdom, green for success and bright red for confidence, but you may associate these attributes with quite different colours. If you use the ones I say, the spell won't work for you as the colours won't stimulate the same meaning in your subconscious and the power will be mis-focused. Always study what recognised experts say and then decide for yourself.

A word here about circle-casting. Many Witches do this before any working, and many do not. Some traditions work within a square or other symbolic shape. There is no right or wrong. You can cast a circle if you want for protection, as a sacred space, to enclose and concentrate the power you are raising, to link together several practitioners working together, or for any other reason. But I would also point out that, if you work alone, you may find it easier and more natural to simply protect and bless yourself. Some religions sanctify a building for worship such as a church or temple, others practice in places they already consider to be naturally sacred such as a grove of trees, if you're a pantheist you will believe that you are already sacred and so is everything in the world so you won't need a special sacred place. Again, the key here is to understand the meaning behind your actions so that you don't feel you have to do one thing or another, but you will feel what the right thing is for you to do.

Candle magic and sympathetic magic are two common methods of using magic which require a small amount of equipment. For candle magic, you need candles in appropriate colours for your aims which you can anoint with appropriate diluted essential oils which also reflect your aims if you want.

Remember that essential oils can be flammable, so be careful if you do this. You may also wish to scratch symbols or initials onto the candle to represent your intentions.

Exercise

- A candle spell for general well-being. Select a new, unused candle in the colour which you associate with your general well-being and happiness. If you wish to anoint it (rub it with oils) or add a symbol to it, decide which will be most appropriate for your aims. Sit quietly and close your eyes while holding the candle. Concentrate on your intention i.e. that you will be well and happy, while you hold the candle or anoint it or scratch on the symbol. When you feel that you have transmitted your intention, open your eyes and staying focused on your intention, light the candle. Sit and watch it burn for as long as you wish, and then let it burn down. Don't leave a lit candle unattended, in an empty room, or where pets or children may have access to it.

Sympathetic magic means using one item as a substitute for another – generally these items will have something in common so as to be representative of one another. This is the basis for using dolls to represent people in some forms of magic. It can also mean using other things which seem to you to be appropriate – for example using a seed in a fertility spell. There are all sorts of methods of spellcraft which you may want to try along these lines, for example, burying an effigy of something you want to get rid of from your life or writing down something you wish to get rid of and then burning it. You can find ideas for these kinds of spells in any beginner's book on magic, but they will be more effective if you sit down and really think hard about what you want to do and then use your own ideas. This may seem difficult to start with, so by all means get ideas from other people, but don't just use them verbatim – adapt them to be personal to you and spend time thinking about the ideas behind the spell so that next time you can improve on it by writing your own.

You may well find, after some practise and experience, that you wish to concentrate on one particular form of magic and learn it thoroughly. If you are using more complicated methods, such as herbal healing or High Ritual magic, then you will need to study other people's writings on the subject much more thoroughly as it is important to get it right. You may even decide that you don't wish to cast spells very often and prefer to do meditation and visualisation work, or to concentrate on a healing art such as aromatherapy. You may find you have a talent for divination – see if you are drawn to this area by trying out various different methods such as runes, tarot or the I Ching. If you are a highly intuitive person who is often sought out by friends with problems, you may well have a natural leaning towards this kind of work and/or healing.

The main thing is not to get too bogged down with the multitude of methods and skills you could learn. By all means give each a try to see which you are most drawn to, but don't try to learn them all thoroughly at once. You don't have be an expert in everything by this time tomorrow! If you are drawn to learning several things, decide which you want to do first and stick to that. Now that you have found your path you will be on it and still learning for the rest of your life. There is no rush. You can very easily overload yourself, become disillusioned and give everything up. Instead, be realistic about the amount of time you have to commit to studying magic and healing and pace yourself accordingly. For example, you could do an evening class in aromatherapy this year and then next year study tarot. As long as you make practical plans and then stick to them, you are not procrastinating you are organising yourself sensibly.

A word about confidence here – there will always be someone else you know who allegedly is a natural medium, can read minds, has visions and all sorts of glamorous skills, whereas you may feel that you have no natural abilities at all. Don't believe it – there are many Witchy talents which are hugely powerful, yet very unobtrusive: healer, teacher, philosopher, parent, friend, daughter, son, life-partner, empath, scholar – many Witches are skilled in one of these rather than being psychic or good at divination. They may seem less showy, but these kinds of quiet, everyday skills make a huge impact on other people and therefore on the world. Believe in yourself!

Joining a Group or Coven

Some solitaries try working with others at some time in their magical lives.Working with others is a real commitment and you should think very hard before deciding you are ready for this. It shouldn't be something you jump into, thinking that you can always back out if it doesn't work out. Looking for a group shouldn't be the first thing you do when setting out on your spiritual path, it should be something you do when you are already quite a way on your journey. Many people look for a group to teach them without realising that you need to have done a lot of work on yourself already before a group can be expected to teach you anything. In particular you should have done all the work that I have already discussed, and all the thinking about your beliefs. You need to know who you are and exactly what you believe before you seek a group – otherwise how can you possibly know what sort of group you are looking for and what you can offer them?

So, you need to be able to offer a group maturity of thought and a definite knowledge of your spiritual beliefs, but what else? On a purely practical level, you need to be able to offer practical commitment. If you were going to join a darts team which plays matches every week, you wouldn't consider joining if you knew you'd probably only be able to make it half the time due to other commitments – you'd know that this wouldn't be fair as they'd be relying on you to play. The same is true of group magic working. Decide how often you can commit to meeting and find a group which meets only this often. There will always be crises in life which mean you have to miss a meeting occasionally, and maybe something in your life will change at some point, such as a new job or baby, which will mean you have to re-think your commitment – but at the outset you need to be sure that you can keep to the level of contact required by the group.

If you would like to work with others or learn from others but feel you can't commit to a group, consider trying to find a more experienced Witch who can act as a one-on-one teacher or mentor. Or else see if you can find a like-minded person who would be a magical partner for occasional workings together. Many people work with their romantic partner and find this a very satisfactory arrangement. There doesn't have to be a hard and fast split between being solitary and working in a group – it can be more of a sliding scale. Even if you don't actually work with anyone else, knowing other Witches and Pagans and being able to discuss points of magical technique or experience is very valuable and can give you helpful pointers. It should always be borne in mind that many traditions regard their magical workings as secret or private and will not discuss them casually or with people outside their own traditions. If you ask someone something and they prefer not to discuss it, don't push it, respect their beliefs.

Safety

When trying to find a group or even just make contact with like-minded individuals, don't leave your common sense at the door. As much as we may wish otherwise, there are unscrupulous and untrustworthy people out there, even in the Witchy world – don't let yourself be a victim. Don't give out your real name, address, phone number or any other real-life details to anyone on the internet. You have no way of knowing if anyone is who they say they are and it is scary to be stalked.

Always try to find out about a group or person from a third party before getting involved or agreeing to meet up. Try asking local groups, people you know from moots or gatherings, or even in your local esoteric bookshop. Unhealthy groups tend to get a reputation. Remember that if you're under eighteen, it is unlikely that any reputable group will accept you, so be very wary of any that state age is not a problem. Reputable covens and groups won't actively recruit so if anyone offers you initiation without you having asked for it, be very wary. Likewise, if there is money or sex involved – this shouldn't be a standard part of any groups activities and if anyone asks you for money (beyond reasonable expenses for travel or equipment) or to take part in sexual activities, then leave and don't go back. Some groups practise ritual nudity and it is up to you if you find this acceptable or not. It should never be sprung on you as a surprise or be something you feel forced into. If you're comfortable with it, fine, but if you're not, try another group which practises clothed.

If you're trying to find an individual teacher or a course of some kind, the same precautions apply. The more money it costs, the less value it is likely to have. Plus, be very wary of getting into an unhealthy reliance on one particular person. Good teachers or mentors will actively encourage you to seek your own answers and will not expect you merely to parrot their own beliefs. Anyone who objects to you questioning their teaching must be seen as suspect.

If you're meeting up with a potential group or teacher for the first time, choose a public place, such as a pub, tell people where you're going and who you're meeting and take someone along with you. Never go to a stranger's house for any reason and certainly never go alone to meet strangers.

Be wary of who you give your trust to – it can be very disillusioning to trust a person or group and then have that trust betrayed. Protect yourself physically as well as emotionally and spiritually. Your motto should be 'if in doubt, leave'. This is particularly true the younger you are. Some teens may try to find groups or teachers without telling their parents what they are doing as they feel their parents disapprove of their beliefs. If you do this you are putting yourself at risk – secrecy aids unscrupulous groups, and if they know you are desperate to find a group, they may realise you will go along with just about anything in order not to lose your membership of this one. Don't put yourself in this position. If you really have found your true path then waiting a few years in order to pursue it safely will not kill you. There is much you can do alone to prepare yourself in the meantime. When you are ready, a chance will come.

White and Black Magic

I haven't mentioned these terms so far, for the simple reason that I don't believe there's any such thing as white or black magic outside tabloid newspapers. Magic is the force of will which individuals can project to affect the outside world. Like electricity, it is not by nature good or evil, but can be put to both ends depending on the user and the viewpoint. Generally, people say they use white magic when they are trying to reassure someone that they are a good person and that they practise magic ethically. People who say they use black magic can mean one of two things: either they use magic unethically and for selfish reasons and to hurt other people, or that they use the power of their darker emotions to practise their magic. These two things are entirely different. Those who profess the former are people to avoid – after all, who would want to associate with someone who was only out for themselves and would not hesitate to harm people? People who talk about being into 'black' magic quite often also profess to being Satanists or to worship demons. There is often a certain level of ignorance on their parts and a desire to shock, as these different beliefs do not go together. Satan is part of the Christian pantheon and therefore is not worshipped or even believed in by Pagans or Witches, and demons are historically merely a different form of spirit, originally a disembodied soul. There is therefore nothing particularly shocking about a Witch working with such entities.

Harnessing magical power through the darker side of life is an entirely different concept and a valid one, although one to be used with care. We all have a dark side, those emotions we would rather forget about and sweep under the carpet: anger, jealousy, resentment, envy. Some of us enjoy the sleazy glamour of the darker things in life: the night, the moon, alcohol, obsession, blood, death and velvet clothing (!) – such as epitomised by the Goth lifestyle. Some people classify desire and lust as one of the darker emotions, and many people enjoy taking intense experiences to the outer limits. Anyone who has ever experienced any of these emotions can be in no doubt of their power, and if they can be harnessed safely, they can be used to very good effect in magical workings. Just as we accept destruction in Nature as part of the cycle of life and as a necessary step in the path to rebirth, our darker sides can be used for positive ends. We have probably all done so unconsciously at one time or another. Have you ever been really angry about something? So angry that you became positively energetic and rushed around in a flurry of activity getting something done, probably muttering 'I'll show them' under your breath as you did it? Then you have already harnessed your dark side.

It is very important to acknowledge your own darker aspects, whether or not you wish to work with them. You can only be ambushed unexpectedly by them if you try to deny their existence. If you know they are there, what they are, and in what situations they tend to emerge, you can be ready for them – either to diffuse them or to harness them. As with all things, an interest in the darker side of life can be taken too far. It should be obvious that an interest in death which is taken too far can have fatal consequences, just as an interest in using alcohol or drugs to alter states of consciousness can have seriously detrimental effects on mental and physical health (and some may be illegal). The darker side may be attractive and powerful, but it is not an easy option and should not be utilised without due caution. It also lends itself to exploitation by unscrupulous practitioners eager to control naïve newcomers. If a potential teacher, mentor or group tells you they practise dark magic, make sure they define in detail exactly what they do and how, and what they will expect of you, before getting involved. It may seem glamorous to take part in a rite of blood oath, but it is by no means glamorous to catch hepatitis or HIV. Remember the dividing line between what is romantic in fantasy and what is deadly in reality.

If you are drawn to dark magic, don't forget to keep a balance in your life. If you like the night and the moon, try a midday sun working sometimes. If you are interested in death and decay, don't forget about the rebirth that follows.

Science

If you ask the average person in the street if they believe in magic, they will probably laugh and reply that believing in magic is a medieval idea or one associated with ignorance and superstition, certainly not something for the Western world in the twenty-first century. And yet, how many of these same people will still subconsciously use magic – for example making a wish as they blow out their birthday cake candles, or avoid planning an important interview for Friday 13th? The word 'magic' has become laughable, but the concept is still alive and well in people's minds. If you ask the same average person in the street if they feel there is some force in the universe pushing for good and for order, or if they believe that sometimes things happen which cannot be explained by current science, they may well answer 'yes'.

In the past two hundred years, the rise in science and technology has been unprecedented and meteoric. So much has been discovered about the natural world, the body and the whole universe that it can seem that there is no unexplored or unexplained territory for religion to inhabit. I would argue that this view of science and religion as competing, with science having emerged as the rational option, is wrong. In fact, I would go further and say that science itself is magical. Anyone who has ever looked under a microscope to see living cells dividing must agree, or anyone who has ever seen a baby moving inside themselves on an ultrasound scan, or anyone who has ever made instantaneous contact with someone on the other side of the planet by phone or internet. We forget how magical these applications of science are because they are labelled as 'technology'.

Religion and science have come to be regarded as enemies in the Western world due to the clash between Christianity and biology over the issue of evolution, which can be held to contradict the authorised biblical tradition of creation. But in many other countries, there has been no such conflict between religion and science – it is not seen in many Islamic countries for example. This is because religion and science are both held to be important disciplines which each hold the key to different parts of life. For example, biology and chemistry may help us explain how the brain works but they don't explain why we've each got a unique sense of humour, and we don't expect them to. The kind of question which relates to the value we place on individual human lives is in the religious arena. Science can discover how the universe started, but religion asks the question 'who, if anyone, created it and why?' Science may find a gene which predisposes someone to antisocial behaviour, but religion asks 'what is the nature of evil?' The two disciplines should be complementary -

sometimes knowledge from one discipline can illuminate the other. For example, the spiritual belief about everything being interconnected has been echoed by current physics research into Chaos Theory and quantum mechanics.

The only clash between religion and science comes when people hold their scientific views as if they were a fundamentalist religion i.e. if they dismiss the possibility of other theories and hypotheses, if they cling to particular beliefs even in the face of contradictory evidence, and if they try to 'convert' other people to their way of thinking. On the other hand, holding religious beliefs in a scientific way can be positively beneficial in that you will think carefully about why you believe each thing and test each belief logically. This can only be a good thing as it will help to order your mind and increase your sense of self. At the end of the day, both religion and science rely on faith, as we come to borders of knowledge past which we have no certain evidence. As long as we use sense, logic and reasoning up to this point, whatever we hypothesise beyond it has a good chance of being based in reality. And as long as we are open-minded enough to re-evaluate beliefs in the light of new evidence, then both science and religion should benefit.

End of Chapter Relaxation

Think of the favourite holiday you ever took – it doesn't have to be the most exotic or the most recent, just the holiday that you actually enjoyed the most. Why did you enjoy that holiday as much as you did? Was it the location, the weather, the company, the food? Was it things you did or didn't do? Was it the atmosphere, the way you felt at the time? Whatever it was, try to recreate it for one day, now, at home. Get in appropriate food or music, turn the heating up and put on a swimming costume. Invite round the people you went on the holiday with and involve them. Put aside your usual responsibilities for one day and lounge around reading a holiday novel. Watch a film that is set in the same location as your holiday and get out your photos of the holiday. Try to make that lovely holiday feeling last, and identify exactly what it was about that you enjoyed so much, so that you can recreate the same mood whenever you want to.

Further Reading

Non-fiction
Witchcraft – a Beginner's Guide – Teresa Moorey (1996, Hodder & Stoughton).
A very good basic guide to Witchcraft with some standard guides to magical correspondences, ideas for altars and first rituals.

The Penguin Dictionary of Symbols – Chevalier & Gheerbrant (eds) (1996, Penguin Books).
A good dictionary for checking correspondences, symbols and traditional associations in many different traditions and cultures.

The Field – Lynne McTaggart (2003, Element).
Layman's book about the current merging of physics research and spirituality.

Fiction
Altered States – Paddy Chayefsky (1981, Bantam Books).
Another classic novel on the themes of states of consciousness, what constitutes humanity and what is important in life, as the hero learns how powerful the repercussions can be when you dabble within your own subconscious.

Island – Aldous Huxley (1994, Flamingo).
Not the most famous of Huxley's writings, but a fantastic novel looking at an alternative culture based on esoteric ways of thinking and isolated from modern scientific thought.

Chapter 5
Natural Cycles

Tuning in to natural cycles is at the very heart of Witchcraft. It is what gives us a large part of our power and yet is such a simple idea. It is a long term project though, as cycles change slowly over a long period and we must become attuned to observing them. In this way, we can use power and cast spells according to the prevailing natural cycle rather than against it. This is similar to shooting an arrow into the wind instead of against it – it will fly much further without any more effort on your part. There are three main cycles to become aware of. Firstly there is your own life cycle – what stage of life you are at currently. Secondly there is your immediate surroundings – your sense of place, its history, what it means to you and how you fit in with it. And thirdly, there is the seasonal cycle – the way the year is divided up into different moods.

Your Life Cycle

Your stage of life is completely unique to you and is always changing, albeit ever so slowly. It may be partly based on age and peer group, but it also relies heavily on your personality, maturity, goals in life and beliefs. There are two aspects to your stage in life: the public and the private. The public aspect is those parts of yourself which are obvious to outsiders. For example, this could be the fact that you're at school, or that you've just got married, or that you've just set off to travel for a year. These are very obvious facts about yourself which identify you as at a particular stage in your life. A stranger being told just this one thing about you could probably make a guess at other things about you, such as age or certain personal values. The public aspects of your life cycle are important, but not as important as the private aspects. These are the unique parts of your life cycle which identify you as you. Examples of these private aspects are your emotions and beliefs about things, the kind of person you see yourself as being, the ambitions and goals you have for your life, your thoughts and principles.

The public aspects of your stage of life can affect your life to a huge extent merely because they provide the assumptions upon which other people treat you in a certain way. But this aspect will also determine to some extent your particular concerns of the moment and what kind of person you may feel comfortable with. For example, if you're sixteen years old and currently at school, it is a fair bet that a large part of your time and energy is engaged with thoughts of GCSEs, career choices and thoughts over whether you will leave school or go on to college. You will probably have a lot of friends who are of the same age and stage as you, and maybe friends who are more than a couple of years younger will start to seem babyish, and their concerns more trivial than your own. Similarly, if you have just started at university, you may find your life diverging quite considerably from friends of the same age who have just started work. Your 'worlds' will be very different and it may be harder to maintain a friendship when you have less in common. Getting married or having a baby can entirely change your social circle and support system, just as it can cause your family to treat you differently – as if you have finally become a member of an exclusive club of adults. Changing working patterns to non-conventional hours, or retiring can also mean a huge change in how you see yourself and how others see you, as well as having a huge impact on the amount of time and money you have available for pursuing interests.

Hopefully by now you will begin to see how important these kind of life stages can be for your magical ability and your capacity to commit to studying your craft, learning with a teacher, or joining a group. You need to take into account how much time you realistically have for your magical studies having planned for the other commitments in your life. You also need to think carefully about how much energy you have for giving to other people, and what experiences you have had to bring to your practice. This may be age-related, but it may not be. A teenager may be in a unique position to help other teenagers as s/he will know exactly what kinds of problems and issues are at stake, but equally a teenager who has been through a parental marriage break-up may be well-placed to help an adult going through their own split. Try to capitalise on the strengths and experiences of your own particular life stage when doing magic or healing. Stick to what you know and don't overstretch yourself when taking into account other commitments. Also, don't be too hard on yourself – if you need a break from magical practice in order to cope with a new development in your life cycle, then take one. Although it is important not to let mundane considerations overwhelm your spiritual life, there will be times when you will find it hard on a short-term basis to achieve an adequate balance and you will need to concentrate on one thing for a short time. For example, going through an exam period for GCSEs, A-Levels or degree finals; the first few months with a new baby; the first few weeks of a new job; when you're away from home travelling; after a bereavement.

You can encounter problems which are typical of your public life stage within your Witchcraft practice. For example, many young people find that it is hard for them to be taken seriously, especially when they have new or challenging ideas of how to practise. In their twenties and thirties people may increasingly find their magical practice and spiritual path taking a back seat to other concerns such as studying, career, relationships, children, travelling, other interests. There may be a sense of struggling to juggle everything and dropping one or more of the balls! In their forties and fifties, people may have been practising for a long time and find that they have achieved their immediate goals and think 'what now?' They may be struggling with the issue of what or how to teach their children about their beliefs. They may also consider that the younger generation of Witches do not respect their experience as much as they would hope. In their sixties and seventies and above people may face issues to do with retirement, loss of income, loss of mobility or independence which hit hard their sense of personal identity and power. Carers from agencies such as social services may find it hard to understand your personal beliefs and you may find you have to fight hard to have your beliefs respected in an institutional setting such as hospital or care home.

There are no easy answers to any of these problems, although most will seem easier to cope with if you know someone with similar beliefs going through the same life stage with whom you can discuss appropriate responses. Don't forget that religious beliefs do not have to be set for life. You should constantly re-evaluate your spirituality to check it still fits your sense of who you are as a person. You may find your beliefs change over time and with different circumstances.

The private aspect of your stage of life is going to relate far more to your sense of personal power and the kinds of magical practice and method you learn and experiment with. Hopefully, after working through chapter one you will know yourself a lot better and be much clearer in your own mind as to what kind of person you are. This is pivotal to the private aspect of your stage of life as it will determine what you are trying to achieve, how you deal with life and the workings that you attempt. Are you a level-headed or passionate person, are you an intellectual or practical person, are you a worrier or calm? These personality traits will affect the type of person you feel an immediate bond with and also affect the kind of advice you give people, or the magic you do. If you enjoy studying you may well learn one of the more complicated and in-depth methods of Witchcraft such as herbalism. If you're an intuitive person you may be drawn to something like tarot. If you're a practical person you may find sacred gardening is a natural step. Knowing the general kind of person you are and how you react to things will help immensely in keeping up with the different stages of your life.

We are all tested by life – as many people have said 'no-one ever said it was going to be easy'. Many people of all different religions believe that going through hardships is a form of being tested, baptised or initiated by their deities. As Witches we may or may not believe that but what we should believe is that every trial is a learning opportunity and is trying to teach us something. What we learn and how is up to us, but the main thing is to try to work with the flow of our lives and not against it. Try to learn the lesson life is teaching you, not a different one. For example, don't try to heal others when you need healing yourself. Don't spend all your time at your local college learning herbalism when life is trying to teach you how to keep a marriage together. Don't try to join a coven when life keeps moving you from one place to another. Instead, sit down quietly – literally or metaphorically – and listen to what life is trying to tell you. If you keep losing your job, could it be that your career is not currently going in the right direction? If you're always suffering from ill-health, is something in life out of kilter that you need to put right? If you are trying to learn the tarot but it is not working for you, could it be that you have overlooked some other form of working that is more suited to you? These can be hard lessons to learn. Maybe our true path is not the one we have assumed it was for many years, maybe it is not even the one we wanted it to be. Maybe we have to put aside what we are currently doing in life in order to learn a lesson before being able to go back to it once we have done so. Maybe we have to admit to ourselves that we are not the person we thought we were, or that we wanted to be. Maybe we have to admit we have been lazy, selfish or just guilty of not achieving what we could have if we'd set our minds to it. Sometimes we may know that we are meant to do a certain thing, but we have to learn that it won't be yet. Patience is the hardest lesson to learn for most of us.

The private aspects of our stage of life may change just as much as the public ones. We may adjust our beliefs and principles when we gain new information or new experiences. Doing things such as travelling or having children can entirely change your perspective on a lot of things and you may find that your fundamental aims in life change. As you grow older and fulfil your original ambitions in life, you will come up with new ones based on your own experiences in life. Sometimes a huge shock can show you your true path in life – for example people who lose a loved one to violence or illness and devote their lives to fund-raising or campaigning. Maybe you will suffer an illness or trauma yourself and then find that your path in life is to support others who are suffering similarly.

Most of us will go through life without having to cope with such huge upsets and yet as our role changes and we have more responsibilities, we will find it substantially affecting our own power and how we feel we should use it. We may find that at some times in our life we want to work alone, and at others we feel it is right to work in a group. Try to go with your gut instinct on this and also remember that, if it is the right thing to do, it will happen. Generally when things don't go the way we want them to, we later realise that it wouldn't have been right if they had. This is very hard to accept at the time, but with hindsight things generally work out for the best. Trying to stay in tune with your own personal stage of life, both public and private, will ensure that you feel balanced and that you make the best decisions you can.

Exercise

• To find out your personal life stage – if you're in any doubt – simply answer these questions. When you meet new people and they ask you what you do, what do you say? At school, a student, your job title, unemployed, full-time parent, retired? What other public roles do you have? As well as being yourself, you may be someone's boy/girlfriend, husband/wife, mother/father, son/daughter, sister/brother. What are the roles you play in your life which are important to you but which may be less public? For example, the person your friends come to for advice, the one who can always mend a computer, the one who speaks French or who knows about politics. What activities currently take up the majority of your time? Are these the activities you want to spend the most time doing or are you constantly wishing you could do something else? In answering these questions you should be well on the way to knowing both the public and private aspects of your current stage in life. This is something you should reassess regularly, perhaps as much as once a year or more during periods of great change and upheaval in your life.

Your Environment

Your immediate surroundings effect you a great deal, whether this is consciously or unconsciously. Many people find that certain environments make them feel comfortable and others make them uncomfortable, for example a tidy or untidy house, very hot weather or very cold. The first step towards being in tune with your surroundings is knowing this information about yourself. The second step is then learning more about the environment you have chosen so that you can deliberately choose to fit yourself in further – an environment is after all an active system in its own right which can greatly affect you and can itself be changed by you.

Exercise

• What sort of environment is right for you? These days there is a huge choice of surroundings which we can choose. For example, an old house or a new house, tower block or bungalow, city centre or rural isolation, town suburb or country village, historic centre or new town, near woods or on the coast, on flat land or in the midst of hills, on wetland or land which never floods, north, south, west or east. We have much more choice over the place we live than any generation before us and yet we often seem to make this decision for economic reasons or even purely by chance.

Are you currently living in an environment that suits you or are you constantly going away at weekends to an escape which suits you better, or making plans that in five years you will move to your country idyll? Do you yearn to walk by water in the summer evenings but live in a town miles from the sea and with no river?

Do you love to be surrounded by people or would you prefer that your nearest neighbours were a mile away? Does the sight of grey concrete and tower blocks deaden something inside you or are you invigorated by the life found in a city centre? Do you enjoy living in an old house full of history or do you find the echoes of previous inhabitants unsettling and wish you lived somewhere brand new with no previous impressions?

Often the kind of environment in which we feel happiest is linked to childhood memories – either we want to live in the same kind of place we enjoyed as child, or exactly the opposite. Or perhaps we had childhood dreams of one day having a farm with fields and animals, or of living by the sea. Try to remember what your childhood ideal house/living environment was. Does it still appeal now? Are your dreams practical? After a stressful commute to work, many dream of a rural idyll, but sometimes it is not a practical reality and we would not be happy in that kind of isolation.

If you are still not sure what kind of environment is your ideal, let it stew at the back of your mind for a few days. See if you dream about a particular location, or if a picture pops up during meditation, or draw something and see what comes out.

Many people assume that to be a 'proper' Witch, you must live in the countryside and keep your own chickens. Although this is an entirely valid life choice, there is no such thing as one true way. You can just as easily be a Witch in the middle of the city. What matters is making contact with the spirit of the place in which you live. This doesn't necessarily mean conjuring up a pixie-like guardian, although it may manifest itself in this way to some people, just connecting to the sense of your place. There have been many, many people and animals living on the earth during its millions of years of development and the chances are there is some resonance left from those who have lived, loved and died over this time on the very spot where you are now sitting.

Exercise

• Take some time to meditate on the land where your house now stands. Even if you live on the top floor of a huge tower block, remind yourself that there is earth at its base. Think about the people and animals who may have roamed across this land in times gone by. What might they have been like? What kinds of things were important in their lives? If you could meet them, would you have anything in common? Maybe the fact that you both regard this small piece of ground as home links you across time in some way – how might this affect you now?

What do you know about your current environment? Do you know anything of its history, or the geology of the soil, the kind of climate it typically experiences, how long it has been inhabited by humans? Do you know how old the town is, why it was built on this spot, how its industry has changed over the years? Do you know how old your house is and the kinds of people who may have lived in it over the years? This kind of knowledge helps root us in our particular environment and become a part of the spirit of the place. This in turn then enables us to tap into the natural power of the landscape and work with it instead of trying to work against it, or without even acknowledging it.

You may have studied some of these subjects in primary school, where there is a tendency to do projects on the history of the local area. But we forget as we grow older, or we may have moved to a completely different area, so a bit of research could prove fascinating.

Exercise

- Go to your local library and see what you can find out about your local area. Chances are they will have a small section of books by local authors. Books of old photographs are particularly popular right now, but there will also be more ancient history, especially if your area has had archaeological digs done, or if it has a known Roman history, for example. Once you have discovered a little about your particular area, read up on some of the background history. For example, if you discover that your area was home to Bronze Age settlers, find out a little about this era in order to visualise what the people may have been like and what their concerns were. This will help you to connect further with them. A good tip here is to check out history books from the children's library – they tend to be particularly clear and easy-to-read while giving a good overview of the general facts without getting too bogged down in details.

Once you start researching into your area, you may discover that you feel a special affinity with a specific historical group. Britain is a very mixed bag ethnically having absorbed immigrants and invaders from many different lands, cultures and time periods. You can research the history of your own county and find out such details – you may be surprised.

You may know something about your own ethnic background, or you may just feel drawn to a particular culture or heritage, such as Roman, African or Anglo-Saxon. Don't ignore this, it is an important part of tuning into your environment and can form a large part of your desire to move to or live in a specific area. Many people feel drawn to places such as Ireland or Cornwall and it could well be that they are tuning in to a part of their individual heritage which is originally from that area.

However, don't just assume that because you are drawn to Paganism or Witchcraft then you must have an affinity with the Celtic period – the two things are not synonymous. All things Celtic are very fashionable these days and the term seems to lump together many different peoples who lived far from each other and in different time periods. It is very unlikely that Bronze Age Scots had much in common culturally with Dark Age Cornish people, and yet both have been labelled Celtic. Try to narrow down exactly what it is that you are feeling drawn to and avoid the cultural stereotypes which can mislead you. Just to remind you, the various ancient ethnicities/cultures/labels in Britain include: Scottish (Highland and Lowland), English, Irish, Welsh, Cornish, Saxon, Anglo-Saxon, Viking, Norman, Breton, Jute and Roman. More recent additions include various African and Caribbean peoples, Indian and Asian cultures and the British emigrants to Australia and America. In short, a list could never be exhaustive as the culture and ethnic background of the British Isles includes so many different cultures and ethnic backgrounds and the same is true of most other countries.

Although you may not wish to practise a re-creationist or revivalist kind of religion, finding out about a culture and historical period which you feel personally drawn to can be very enriching for your sense of yourself and your sense of family. Don't get too hung up on culture as a divisive force however – remember that the further we look back, the more we all have in common and it's likely that we all evolved from a common and very small gene pool. This is an exercise in rootedness not racism.

The Seasonal Cycle

The seasonal cycle is one of the easiest ways to start your practise of Witchcraft and one of the most interesting. The longer you do it, the more you will notice and the more interesting it will become. Much of it will depend on where you live and the climate there, and it can be fascinating to compare notes with a friend who lives in another part of the country or on higher or lower ground than you do, to see the differences even within relatively small distances. Things to start noting in your diary could be:

• When you see the first snowdrops of spring;

• When your grass first needs cutting;

• The first leaf to fall from the trees and the last;

• Whether it snows;

• When the first blossom appears.

Many people notice when the air first starts to smell of spring or of autumn, and observing whether the squirrels have been active over the winter can tell you how mild it has been. Once you have built up such observations over a couple of years, you will start being able to know for sure whether the spring is early or late for your area this year, and whether the summer has lasted unusually long, or if the winter has been unusually harsh. Such knowledge helps us attune to our surroundings and adjust our lives accordingly. For example, knowing that the winter has been unusually long and cold means that we will expect an increase in coughs and colds, and that people may be more than usually low after the long dark season. In these circumstances we would know what herbal remedies to prepare and stockpile, the kinds of emotional support that people will require from us, the kinds of foods which are appropriate to nourish us, and the kinds of magic that are suited to the mood of the season.

For some people, observing their own particular seasonal pattern is enough to enable them to celebrate and attune to natural cycles. However, some people like a predetermined calendar of specific dates to celebrate, and this is where the Wheel of the Year comes in.

The most common Wheel of the Year celebrated by Witches and Pagans is the Celtic one, although it is unlikely that all the very different Celtic cultures would have celebrated precisely the same dates for seasonal rituals – the beginning of summer in Cornwall is likely to be on a very different date than the start of the summer in the Scottish Highlands!

The dates for the Celtic festivals are usually taken as the following:

Samhain - 31st October (New Year)

Solstice - 22nd December (Midwinter)

Imbolc - 2nd February

Equinox - 21st March

Beltane - 30th April

Solstice - 22nd June (Midsummer)

Lughnasadh - 31st July

Equinox - 21st September

There is a lot of controversy about different spellings, pronunciations and origins of all of these festivals, although it is impossible to know for sure about any of them. They may be of ancient provenance or relatively recent date, but the important thing to remember is that they are meant to be a guide to observance of the land and its seasonal changes. Don't become a slave to a particular date if it seems to have no meaning for the land where you live. A good example of this is the way Australian Pagans are reinventing their own Wheel of the Year to fit in with a Southern Hemisphere seasonal cycle or looking into their own aboriginal seasonal stories and myths.

If the Celtic Wheel doesn't appeal, there are various other seasonal festival calendars to look into. For example, the Anglo-Saxon month names give a lot of insight into their festival year and the seasonal rites which were important to them:

Æfterra Geola (month after winter solstice)

Solmonath (sun or cake month)

Hrethmonath (month of Hretha)

Eostremonath (month of Eostre)

Thrimilci (month of three milkings of cows)

Ærra Litha (month before summer solstice)

Æfterra Litha (month after summer solstice)

Weodmonath (month of weeds)

Haligmonath (month of offerings)

Winterfylleth (first winter full moon)

Blotmonath (month of sacrifice)

Ærra Geola (month before winter solstice)

Again, it must be pointed out that authenticity is very much in question here, despite meticulous recordings of these names and suggested interpretations by the medieval monk Bede. But the picture emerges of an agricultural culture, very close to the land and for whom the solstices were very important. The Anglo-Saxon New Year began the day after the winter solstice, rather than Samhain as in the Celtic calendar, and it is up to you to decide which period has more resonance for you as a time of new beginnings.

It can also be seen that the Anglo-Saxon calendar is less precise for dates than the Celtic – the different periods of the year merge into one another with a whole month named after the appropriate festival for the time of year. This can allow more scope for observing the actual landscape and timing your own celebrations and observations to fit the current weather, climate and your own feelings about the tide of the season.

The Roman festival calendar was much more complicated –
obviously it varied widely over the time-span of the Roman
Empire and as it adapted itself to the different countries
conquered. There were also festivals which were much more
important in the countryside than the towns and vice versa,
plus a multitude of local and household deities to be
celebrated. However, here is an approximate guide to some of
the main festivals (dates adjusted to modern equivalents):

New Year - 15th March

Liberalia - 17th March (festival of fertile crops and
    vineyards)

Floralia - 28th April – 3rd May (festival of bloom)

Festival of Vesta - June

Consualia - 21st August (festival of Consus/chariot-
    racing event)

Meditrinalia - 11th October (festival for the wine crop)

Saturnalia - 17th December (festival of sowing in the
    countryside and partying in the towns!)

Lupercalia - February (festival of fertility)

If you are a Witch practising in the city, then celebrating a
Roman urban calendar of festivals may feel more natural to
you than a calendar based on agricultural dates of which you
may know little. There is also a lot of wine involved in Roman
festivities which may help sway you towards their annual
cycle!

Obviously there are a great many more festivals based on natural cycles from different cultures. It is a good idea to research at least those for the cultures you feel particularly drawn to before you decide which, if any, to celebrate on a ongoing basis. Some people who use Egyptian, Sumerian or Babylonian pantheons are similarly drawn to using their annual festival cycles. However, beware of choosing a cycle which is completely at odds with the actual seasonal cycles of the place you live, otherwise you may find yourself celebrating and practising inappropriately for the landscape you are in, which will affect the power you are able to put into the magic.

So, what is appropriate magic for the time of year? Again, this is something you will practise, experience and decide for yourself, but a general guide for a Witch in the Northern hemisphere might be:

• New Year – a time for planing new beginnings or divination;

• Winter – a time for drawing in on yourself and having an inner focus, consolidating anything new learned during the year, conserving strength and resting with family or friends. Apart from New Year, not a great time for new projects, but a very good time to rid yourself of things, beliefs or hang-ups which are holding you back;

• Spring – the ideal time for new ideas, jobs and projects in general, creativity and new beginnings. This is a good time for cleaning the house from top to bottom and generally making a fresh start in mind and body. Spells to enhance confidence will be good now;

• Summer – you can afford to coast a little now, your new projects should all be well-established now and looking to bear fruit shortly. There is still time to start new things, but generally everything you do now should be bursting with positivity, such as healing.

• Autumn – a good time for finishing things which are past their sell-by date, including jobs, tasks, projects or relationships. Also for re-assessing the things you want to take with you into the winter and disposing of any excess baggage, physical or emotional. This is also a time of remembering ancestors and dead loved-ones and honouring their memories.

Seasonal cycles can cause much argument about their authenticity or historical credentials, but the main thing not to lose sight of is that they should be personal to you. Some people may choose not to follow the seasons at all but instead make an in-depth study of lunar cycles and use these alone in ascertaining the appropriate time for magic. For those who suffer from Seasonal Affective Disorder or the milder Winter Blues, becoming more aware of the annual solar cycle may help you to cope. Some people may be drawn to performing magic at night, while others prefer the daytime. It often seems to be the case that people are drawn either to the sun or moon mainly and this can affect the type of magic practised. For example different traditions view sun and moon as male and female. The moon has a very obvious monthly cycle whereas the sun's cycle is more subtle. The sun may be more prominent in hot places whereas the moon may play a larger role in more northerly countries where it is dark a good deal of the winter.

Some people may protest that I have talked a lot about being 'drawn to' particular things in this chapter – what do you do if you don't feel particularly drawn to anything specific? This is where the hard work and patience comes in – you need to spend time observing until you do feel an attraction to a particular area. If you try things randomly with no thought as to whether they are suited to you, you will be short-changing yourself as you won't work to the best of your ability and consequently your confidence will wane. For some people, it may take years of work on this area before they feel ready to take the next step. This is fine. You shouldn't measure your progress by whatever anyone else says or does, but only by your own feelings. As long as you are on the right path and heading in the right direction, then don't worry how long it takes you. The journey is at least as important as the destination and we shouldn't be in such a hurry to arrive that we miss out on the scenery along the way.

The seasonal cycle is also a great learning tool for children and young people. If you want to bring your children up Pagan or even just instil in them an appreciation of nature, then seasonal cycles are an ideal way to start. Going for walks around the park and bringing home leaves or feathers, watching when particular flowers are in bloom, or noticing the kinds of weather typical to each season are all things which small children enjoy doing. Older children can make up scrapbooks of seeds they can find, or take photographs of the garden over different months and then compare them. Teenagers and young people who have made their own choice to study Witchcraft often find that reputable teachers and covens won't take them under the age of eighteen, and then become frustrated at the delay in starting their practise. But in reality there is no need to delay, as becoming attuned to all the cycles mentioned in this chapter is the start of a practice of Witchcraft and is vital to underpin all other knowledge – and can be done by everyone irrespective of age.

Witchcraft is, at heart, an earth-honouring way of life and yet many people attempt to practise it without even being aware of their immediate surroundings, let alone the earth as a whole. This is entirely missing the point of Witchcraft and emphasises once again that Witchcraft in the real world is not the glamorous, high-kicking, demon-vanquishing exercise that is portrayed in fictional dramas. Witchcraft in the real world is down-to-earth and practical. It is knowing about life and how it works. It is appreciating natural things and becoming attuned to them. It is learning and becoming wise.

End of Chapter Relaxation

As Witches, we are accustomed to using our senses, but touch is one sense which is often overlooked and can bring a great deal of pleasure. For this relaxation exercise, I want you to explore your sense of touch and draw in its benefits. There are many ways to do this. Firstly, if you have a partner, family or friends close by - become more tactile. I don't mean go overboard and hug complete strangers, just people you know well and care about. Touching another person in a positive way (as long as they are okay with it) can make you both feel loved and strong. Have you forgotten how to hug? Do you ever cuddle your parents or your children? If you and your partner have been together for a while, have you forgotten how to spend an evening on the sofa cuddled up together? Rediscover the power and comfort of hugging.

Don't overlook pets. Obviously some pets are more cuddly than others, and a goldfish or iguana isn't going to enjoy an evening on your lap, but if you have cats or dogs or other animals which enjoy stroking, grooming or just sitting close to you, spend some time doing this and notice how good it can make you feel.

To take the exercise further, experiment with fabrics. Go to the fabric department of a shop and spend a while touching the various different kinds of cloth. Which do you like the feel of and which do you dislike? Do you like things to be smooth or furry; cool to the touch or warming; simple or luxurious? How many of the fabrics you like do you have in your home? Could you incorporate more of them in your decorations and clothing? For example in cushions, curtains, bedspreads, sofa covers. Are there particular fabrics that you would like to wear next to your skin, or those you would like to avoid? Is your home the temperature you would like it to be? Spend some time creating a haven for your sense of touch and then revel in the comfort this can bring for you.

Further Reading

Non-fiction

Children's Encyclopaedia of British History – Brian Skoyles (1996, Kingfisher Books)
Clear and concise overview of British history from the first Stone-Age people right up to the present day. Great for children and good refresher for adults!

This Sceptred Isle: 55BC-1901 – Christopher Lee (1997, BBC Consumer Publishing)
Aimed more at adults, this book is based on the popular BBC Radio 4 series and covers the people and characters who have influenced British history from the Romans to the death of Queen Victoria.

DK Eyewitness Guides: Tree – David Burnie (1998, Dorling Kindersley)
A great book to have with you on a nature walk to help you identify and recognise trees. It is part of a series which includes plants and flowers.

The Real Witches' Kitchen – Kate West (2002, Thorsons)
A really useful reference book to have, this book gives recipes for seasonal food, oils, lotions, soaps, herbal remedies and much more, both sacred and mundane. It really helps to start you on the path to becoming more aware of natural ingredients and how to use them.

Home: The Story of Everyone Who Ever Lived in Our House – Julie Myerson (2004, Flamingo).
The story of a family who researched their home and found fascinating histories of past inhabitants.

Organisations
BTCV - British Trust for Conservation Volunteers
36 St Mary's Street, Wallingford, Oxfordshire, OX10 0EU
01491 821600
www.btcv.org
With many local branches, the BTCV co-ordinates local
conservation efforts as well as national, and organises
national and international conservation working holidays. A
great way to take more interest in your local environment and
get more hands-on experience with the natural world.

A Final Word

This is my view of Witchcraft, what it means to me, and an example of how to practise it. What I hope I have put across in this book is that every single Witch should think very hard about what it means to them and then practise in their own way. I'm not advocating ignorance or an easy option, on the contrary, I believe that every Witch should make it their lifelong mission to learn, accumulate knowledge and wisdom, think deeply about their beliefs and actions, and be prepared to make sacrifices for them.

To be a Witch you need to be disciplined, you need to be self-aware and constantly questioning in order to know yourself better. I believe you should be happy to take responsibility for your own actions, and also to take on some responsibility for the state of your community, your environment, and the world. You need to be down-to-earth, have common sense and be prepared to use your skills to help those around you.

I don't use tools, poetry or ritual in my practise, but I'm not saying that you shouldn't. What I am saying is that whether you do or do not, you should know the reasons for your choice and have made the choice logically and freely after deep thought. Don't fall into the trap of believing that you need a particular item because you read it in a book, or because someone told you that you couldn't be a proper Witch without it. Question everything until you are satisfied with the response – don't be happy with being told it's because 'it's always been done that way' or because a particular person said so. Rejoice in the differences of practice between yourself and fellow-Witches. Variety and discussion is the life-blood of any belief-system. Dogmatise and institutionalise any belief and it becomes stale. Be passionate and strong about your beliefs, but tolerant of other views. We can always learn from other people, no matter how much we may disagree with their views at first.

Don't rush to do everything at once – take your time to learn things in a logical order and at a slower pace. Enjoy the journey, don't rush to be an expert in everything. Use the time to make friends and contacts at the same stage as you, those more experienced you can learn from, and those less experienced can learn from you. Think everything through carefully and discuss interesting points with others. Don't take things for granted. You don't have to be a beginner to benefit from these things, it is easy to become 'stuck' in life, to feel blocked or to have a crisis of faith. If this happens, don't panic, simply start again from the beginning and gradually work everything out again. Each time you have to do this, your beliefs will emerge the stronger for it.

Be confident in your own beliefs. Many books advocate a Wicca-based practice as the 'only' or the 'proper' way of being a Witch. This is not the case – there are many different ways of doing things and this can include rituals or not, circle-casting or not, tools or not, and covens or not. Maybe you read tarot or maybe you are dedicated parent – both are equally valid spiritual paths utilising your Witchcraft skills. Don't let anyone tell you that you are doing it wrong. Look deep inside yourself and know you are doing it the right way for you. This is all that matters.

Above all, enjoy it! Witchcraft should not be a po-faced, deadly serious practice. There should be laughter and joy, reward and satisfaction. It should help you to feel in tune with yourself, your loved-ones and your surroundings, and at peace within your own mind and soul. It can be a help and solace in times of stress and grieving, and a source of deep contentment at all times.

Be happy.

FREE DETAILED CATALOGUE

Capall Bann is owned and run by people actively involved in many of the areas in which we publish. A detailed illustrated catalogue is available on request, SAE or International Postal Coupon appreciated. **Titles can be ordered direct from Capall Bann, post free in the UK** (cheque or PO with order) or from good bookshops and specialist outlets.

A Breath Behind Time, Terri Hector
Angels and Goddesses - Celtic Christianity & Paganism, M. Howard
Arthur - The Legend Unveiled, C Johnson & E Lung
Astrology The Inner Eye - A Guide in Everyday Language, E Smith
Auguries and Omens - The Magical Lore of Birds, Yvonne Aburrow
Asyniur - Womens Mysteries in the Northern Tradition, S McGrath
Beginnings - Geomancy, Builder's Rites & Electional Astrology, Nigel Pennick
Between Earth and Sky, Julia Day
Book of the Veil , Peter Paddon
Caer Sidhe - Celtic Astrology and Astronomy, Michael Bayley
Call of the Horned Piper, Nigel Jackson
Can't Sleep, Won't Sleep, Linga Louisa Dell
Carnival of the Animals, Gregor Lamb
Cat's Company, Ann Walker
Celtic Faery Shamanism, Catrin James
Celtic Faery Shamanism - The Wisdom of the Otherworld, Catrin James
Celtic Lore & Druidic Ritual, Rhiannon Ryall
Celtic Sacrifice - Pre Christian Ritual & Religion, Marion Pearce
Celtic Saints and the Glastonbury Zodiac, Mary Caine
Circle and the Square, Jack Gale
Come Back To Life, Jenny Smedley
Compleat Vampyre - The Vampyre Shaman, Nigel Jackson
Creating Form From the Mist - The Wisdom of Women in Celtic Myth and
    Culture, Lynne Sinclair-Wood
Crystal Clear - A Guide to Quartz Crystal, Jennifer Dent
Crystal Doorways, Simon & Sue Lilly
Crossing the Borderlines - Guising, Masking & Ritual Animal Disguise in the
    European Tradition, Nigel Pennick
Dragons of the West, Nigel Pennick
Earth Dance - A Year of Pagan Rituals, Jan Brodie
Earth Harmony - Places of Power, Holiness & Healing, Nigel Pennick
Earth Magic, Margaret McArthur
Egyptian Animals - Guardians & Gateways of the Gods, Akkadia Ford

Eildon Tree (The) Romany Language & Lore, Michael Hoadley
Enchanted Forest - The Magical Lore of Trees, Yvonne Aburrow
Eternal Priestess, Sage Weston
Eternally Yours Faithfully, Roy Radford & Evelyn Gregory
Everything You Always Wanted To Know About Your Body, Chris Thomas & D Baker
Face of the Deep - Healing Body & Soul, Penny Allen
Fairies and Nature Spirits, Teresa Moorey
Fairies in the Irish Tradition, Molly Gowen
Familiars - Animal Powers of Britain, Anna Franklin
Flower Wisdom, Katherine Kear
Fool's First Steps, (The) Chris Thomas
Forest Paths - Tree Divination, Brian Harrison, Ill. S. Rouse
From Past to Future Life, Dr Roger Webber
Gardening For Wildlife Ron Wilson
God Year, The, Nigel Pennick & Helen Field
Goddess on the Cross, Dr George Young
Goddess Year, The, Nigel Pennick & Helen Field
Goddesses, Guardians & Groves, Jack Gale
Handbook For Pagan Healers, Liz Joan
Handbook of Fairies, Ronan Coghlan
Healing Book, The, Chris Thomas and Diane Baker
Healing Homes, Jennifer Dent
Healing Journeys, Paul Williamson
Healing Stones, Sue Philips
Herb Craft - Shamanic & Ritual Use of Herbs, Lavender & Franklin
Hidden Heritage - Exploring Ancient Essex, Terry Johnson
Hub of the Wheel, Skytoucher
In Search of Herne the Hunter, Eric Fitch
Inner Celtia, Alan Richardson & David Annwn
Inner Mysteries of the Goths, Nigel Pennick
Inner Space Workbook - Develop Thru Tarot, C Summers & J Vayne
Intuitive Journey, Ann Walker Isis - African Queen, Akkadia Ford
Journey Home, The, Chris Thomas
Kecks, Keddles & Kesh - Celtic Lang & The Cog Almanac, Bayley
Language of the Psycards, Berenice
Legend of Robin Hood, The, Richard Rutherford-Moore
Lid Off the Cauldron, Patricia Crowther
Light From the Shadows - Modern Traditional Witchcraft, Gwyn
Living Tarot, Ann Walker
Lore of the Sacred Horse, Marion Davies
Lost Lands & Sunken Cities (2nd ed.), Nigel Pennick
Magic of Herbs - A Complete Home Herbal, Rhiannon Ryall
Magical Guardians - Exploring the Spirit and Nature of Trees, Philip Heselton
Magical History of the Horse, Janet Farrar & Virginia Russell
Magical Lore of Animals, Yvonne Aburrow
Magical Lore of Cats, Marion Davies

118

Magical Lore of Herbs, Marion Davies
Magick Without Peers, Ariadne Rainbird & David Rankine
Masks of Misrule - Horned God & His Cult in Europe, Nigel Jackson
Medicine For The Coming Age, Lisa Sand MD
Medium Rare - Reminiscences of a Clairvoyant, Muriel Renard
Menopausal Woman on the Run, Jaki da Costa
Mind Massage - 60 Creative Visualisations, Marlene Maundrill
Mirrors of Magic - Evoking the Spirit of the Dewponds, P Heselton
Moon Mysteries, Jan Brodie
Mysteries of the Runes, Michael Howard
Mystic Life of Animals, Ann Walker
New Celtic Oracle The, Nigel Pennick & Nigel Jackson
Oracle of Geomancy, Nigel Pennick
Pagan Feasts - Seasonal Food for the 8 Festivals, Franklin & Phillips
Patchwork of Magic - Living in a Pagan World, Julia Day
Pathworking - A Practical Book of Guided Meditations, Pete Jennings
Personal Power, Anna Franklin
Pickingill Papers - The Origins of Gardnerian Wicca, Bill Liddell
Pillars of Tubal Cain, Nigel Jackson
Places of Pilgrimage and Healing, Adrian Cooper
Planet Earth - The Universe's Experiment, Chris Thomas
Practical Divining, Richard Foord
Practical Meditation, Steve Hounsome
Practical Spirituality, Steve Hounsome
Psychic Self Defence - Real Solutions, Jan Brodie
Real Fairies, David Tame
Reality - How It Works & Why It Mostly Doesn't, Rik Dent
Romany Tapestry, Michael Houghton
Runic Astrology, Nigel Pennick
Sacred Animals, Gordon MacLellan
Sacred Celtic Animals, Marion Davies, Ill. Simon Rouse
Sacred Dorset - On the Path of the Dragon, Peter Knight
Sacred Grove - The Mysteries of the Forest, Yvonne Aburrow
Sacred Geometry, Nigel Pennick
Sacred Nature, Ancient Wisdom & Modern Meanings, A Cooper
Sacred Ring - Pagan Origins of British Folk Festivals, M. Howard
Season of Sorcery - On Becoming a Wisewoman, Poppy Palin
Seasonal Magic - Diary of a Village Witch, Paddy Slade
Secret Places of the Goddess, Philip Heselton
Secret Signs & Sigils, Nigel Pennick
A Seeker's Guide To Past Lives, Paul Williamson
Seeking Pagan Gods, Teresa Moorey
Self Enlightenment, Mayan O'Brien
Spirits of the Air, Jaq D Hawkins
Spirits of the Water, Jaq D Hawkins
Spirits of the Fire, Jaq D Hawkins

Spirits of the Aether, Jaq D Hawkins
Spirits of the Earth, Jaq D Hawkins
Stony Gaze, Investigating Celtic Heads John Billingsley
Stumbling Through the Undergrowth , Mark Kirwan-Heyhoe
Subterranean Kingdom, The, revised 2nd ed, Nigel Pennick
Symbols of Ancient Gods, Rhiannon Ryall
Talking to the Earth, Gordon MacLellan
Talking With Nature, Julie Hood
Taming the Wolf - Full Moon Meditations, Steve Hounsome
Teachings of the Wisewomen, Rhiannon Ryall
The Other Kingdoms Speak, Helena Hawley
Tree: Essence of Healing, Simon & Sue Lilly
Tree: Essence, Spirit & Teacher, Simon & Sue Lilly
Tree Seer, Simon & Sue Lilly
Through the Veil, Peter Paddon
Torch and the Spear, Patrick Regan
Understanding Chaos Magic, Jaq D Hawkins
Vortex - The End of History, Mary Russell
Warp and Weft - In Search of the I-Ching, William de Fancourt
Warriors at the Edge of Time, Jan Fry
Water Witches, Tony Steele
Way of the Magus, Michael Howard
Weaving a Web of Magic, Rhiannon Ryall
West Country Wicca, Rhiannon Ryall
Wheel of the Year, Teresa Moorey & Jane Brideson
Wildwitch - The Craft of the Natural Psychic, Poppy Palin
Wildwood King , Philip Kane
Witches of Oz, Matthew & Julia Philips
Wondrous Land - The Faery Faith of Ireland by Dr Kay Mullin
Working With the Merlin, Geoff Hughes
Understanding Past Lives, Dilys Gater
Understanding Second Sight, Dilys Gater
Understanding Spirit Guides, Dilys Gater
Understanding Star Children, Dilys Gater
The Urban Shaman, Dilys Gater
Your Talking Pet, Ann Walker

FREE detailed catalogue and FREE 'Inspiration' magazine
Contact: Capall Bann Publishing, Auton Farm, Milverton, Somerset, TA4 1NE